Rooted in Christianity
Open to New Light

Timothy Ashworth

grew up in the north of England, the eldest of a large vicarage family. He had left the Church and was working in music and in psychiatric nursing when he found a spiritual orientation with meditation. In his mid-twenties he became a Roman Catholic and trained for the priesthood in Durham. His journey with Friends began when he left the priesthood in 1989 and married Clare in 1990. They now have four children. After being co-warden at Aylesbury Meeting and studying at Oxford, Tim was appointed Biblical Studies tutor at Woodbrooke. He now also co-ordinates Woodbrooke's interfaith courses. His book *Paul's Necessary Sin* was published by Ashgate in 2006.

Alex Wildwood

has been influenced by a wide variety of spiritual paths and traditions. Nominally a Christian at school, he went on to become a Marxist and atheist at college. In his late twenties he discovered the Goddess and began celebrating pagan festivals. He now most readily encounters the Mystery in elemental nature, open-hearted sharing with others and in accepting his own brokenness; he has been called a "neo-Buddhist" and told he has a ministry of vulnerability. A member of the Religious Society of Friends since 1988, he works as a freelance speaker, group facilitator and retreat leader. He gave the 1999 Swarthmore Lecture, published as *A Faith to Call Our Own* (Quaker Home Service).

To Clare Peat,

who first put Fox's *Journal* in my hands, who pursued the opening for us to become wardens at Aylesbury Meeting, who prompted me to apply to teach at Woodbrooke, this is a fruit of our shared encounter with Friends. *T.A.*

To Seren Wildwood,

for holding our domestic life together while I was on the road, for tolerating endlessly shifting deadlines, and for the love that upholds me on all my journeying. *A.W.*

Rooted in Christianity
Open to New Light

Quaker spiritual diversity

Timothy Ashworth
& Alex Wildwood

Pronoun Press in partnership with
Woodbrooke Quaker Study Centre
2009

Published 2009 by Pronoun Press in partnership with
Woodbrooke Quaker Study Centre

Pronoun Press is an imprint of Peter Daniels Publisher Services
35 Benthal Road, London N16 7AR, UK
www.pronounpress.co.uk

Woodbrooke Quaker Study Centre
1046 Bristol Road, Birmingham B29 6LJ
www.woodbrooke.org.uk

ISBN 978-0-9556183-3-8

Contents

Acknowledgements

Many people have contributed to the development of this book. First of all, we express our thanks to all those who participated in the "Rooted in Christianity, Open to New Light" project. Their engagement with the themes we presented to meetings and on residential events at Woodbrooke encouraged us to deepen our dialogue and wrestle further with the issues we write about in these pages. The project itself was part of Woodbrooke's off-site educational programme and we are grateful to Helen Rowlands for her part in making it happen.

After the project, Alex received financial support from the Joseph Rowntree Charitable Trust to co-author a book with Jo Farrow on a new understanding of Quaker spirituality; the model presented in Chapter 3 emerged in the context of his reflections and reading for that book and he is grateful to the Trust for their support. Bob Rowinski provided invaluable help in realising the model with his artwork for the diagrams in Chapter 3.

Other staff members at Woodbrooke have also played key roles in seeing this book into print. In particular, our thanks go to Leonora Wilson for sensitively responding to our struggles at a critical point in the book's evolution, and to Jennie Levin for believing in its value as a resource for Friends in local meetings to use as a follow up to the *Hearts & Minds Prepared* study pack. We appreciated the constructive comments of all the Friends who read our early draft texts and we are thankful too for Lizz Roe's work in seeing the book through to publication.

Our very particular thanks go to our editor, Zélie Gross. Always concerned that we do justice to the potential she saw in the text, she performed an unstinting labour of love in giving so generously of her time and expertise – we gratefully acknowledge that this book would not have reached its present form without her. For all the ways she encouraged us to clarify and strengthen the text we give her our heartfelt thanks.

Introduction

Alex Wildwood and Timothy Ashworth

Alex Wildwood

For almost 300 years, from the earliest days of the Quaker movement in the mid-seventeenth century to some time in the mid-twentieth century, Quakers around the world would have identified themselves as an unmistakably Christian body. Yet in comparatively recent times, Quakers in Britain have become a community that includes a wide spectrum of beliefs and approaches to spiritual practice somehow united under the Quaker umbrella. Although many Friends[1] in Britain today still call themselves Christian, this is often in a highly qualified way – and not necessarily a way that would be recognised by other Christian denominations. More significantly, a considerable number of British Friends would not now describe themselves as Christian in any sense of the word. What accounts for this historic change, and what challenges and opportunities does it present to Friends? Given their very real differences, how do Friends make "unity in diversity" – a much-loved Quaker phrase – more than just an aspiration?

Opening up discussion of such questions is the purpose of the following chapters. They arise out of the experience Timothy Ashworth and I gained from working with Friends between 2001 and 2004 in fifteen area meetings and one regional meeting throughout Britain on a project entitled "Rooted in Christianity, Open to New Light". The aim of this project was to enable groups of Friends to explore the challenges and opportunities of the spiritual diversity now found among British Quakers. During

---

1 "Quaker" and "Friend" are used interchangeably in this book to refer to anyone who is a committed attender of a Quaker meeting.

the project we also offered eight residential events addressing the same issues at Woodbrooke Quaker Study Centre in Birmingham.

The title *Rooted in Christianity, Open to New Light* comes from two phrases in *Quaker Faith & Practice* [2]. This key Quaker document is partly a record of how Friends conduct and govern themselves as a body of worshippers; but it consists mainly of a collection of personal accounts of how members of the Religious Society of Friends witness to their testimonies and translate faith into action in the world, and is revised approximately every thirty years to include new insights and re-evaluate older ones. *Quaker Faith & Practice* begins with a series of "Advices & Queries", which together encapsulate the core values and the practical spirituality of the Quaker way. The project title arose from two of these queries, reflecting two distinct understandings of Quakerism common within Britain Yearly Meeting[3]. Advice no.4 reads:

> The Religious Society of Friends is rooted in Christianity and has always found inspiration in the life and teachings of Jesus. How do you interpret your faith in the light of this heritage? How does Jesus speak to you today? Are you following Jesus' example of love in action? Are you learning from his life the reality and cost of obedience to God? How does his relationship with God challenge and inspire you?

– while Advice no.7 concludes with these three sentences:

> There is inspiration to be found all around us, in the natural world, in the sciences and arts, in our work and friendships, in our sorrows as well as in our joys. Are you open to new light, from whatever source it may come? Do you approach new ideas with discernment?

In our work on the project, my co-author Tim and I spoke for and from these particular perspectives of Quaker faith, addressing the way they indicate the existence today of a range of diverse approaches to Quakerism found among British Friends. Many

2 *Quaker Faith & Practice: The book of Christian discipline of the Yearly Meeting of the Religious Society of Friends (Quakers) in Britain* (London: Britain Yearly Meeting, 4th ed., 2009)
3 The national body of Quakers in Britain.

British Quakers still feel themselves clearly rooted in Christianity either from having been raised as Christian Quakers or from an affirming background of church attendance and religious education in other denominations – as is the case for Tim. However, there are now numbers of Friends who are equally or more influenced by other faith traditions and spiritualities, or who find spiritual inspiration in what science reveals of the universe – as I do. This book explores the fact that, while being rooted in Christianity and being open to the new light of continuing revelation have been essential to Quaker faith from the earliest days, today there is a growing tension between diverse spiritual perspectives within Britain Yearly Meeting; a situation that has only arisen over the last half century. One of the problems we sought to address on the project is that this tension can easily remain hidden and unexpressed among Friends, both through fear of conflict and division and because the silence that is so central to Quaker worship may be masking real differences of which Friends are unaware. As with the original project, this book sets out to name and address this often-unexamined tension and to help Friends consider how different perspectives can co-exist with integrity within one faith community.

Approaching sensitive issues of this kind with groups demands particular care. In order to facilitate what we called "dialogue at depth" in the meetings we visited, we met with each Quaker meeting on a Friday evening and for most of the Saturday, followed by an interval of four to six weeks before everyone gathered again for a second weekend. Authentic sharing between participants was encouraged by including ways of working that engaged both head and heart. So we presented material for discussion and provided reading and follow-up materials to stimulate the mind, but we also facilitated more reflective processes designed to encourage a deeper level of mutual respect and understanding within the worshipping group. One of the ways we did this was by sharing our own stories. We set up a dialogue together, witnessed by the group, in which we spoke of our own spiritual understandings and experience in a way that was always respectful of the other but never made light of our real differences. The structure of this book reflects that process of dialogue, with each of us writing chapters that "listen" to the preceding one. We conclude with two chapters where we each speak from a personal perspective on the essential features of the faith and practice of Friends in a climate of spiritual and religious diversity. By offering these two perspectives we are indicating the ongoing nature of dialogue on the questions we raise in this book.

Once the project had formally ended, but while our residential events were still taking place at Woodbrooke, I started to devise a simple model as an aid to understanding how British Quakers had become such a spiritually diverse community. On being presented with early forms of this model, Friends generally found it helpful as an explanatory device, but also commented that it raised as many questions as it answered! Rather than being discouraged by this response, we came to see it as one of the model's strengths. Our primary intention was always to stimulate discussion and reflection – and the model certainly did that. A further refinement of the model is offered in Chapter 3 in this spirit. We hope readers will find it useful as a way of placing themselves in relationship both to other members of their meetings and to recent historical developments of British Quakerism. This book seeks to make the model and the thinking that has grown out of it more widely available. Although we envisage that, in the main, our readers will be British Friends or Friends in the liberal unprogrammed Quaker tradition elsewhere in the world, we hope that a wider readership also will be interested in the honest struggle of British Quakers to come to terms with issues of spiritual diversity.

It is our intention that something of the flavour of the process of sharing and listening that lay at the heart of the project will be conveyed in the way the book is written and put together. Tim and I begin by introducing ourselves in Chapters 1 and 2, describing our very different backgrounds and spiritual journeys. The model is then outlined in Chapter 3. In Chapters 4 and 5, taking our different faith experiences as our starting points, we examine more broadly the challenges and opportunities of being such a spiritually diverse community. Chapter 6 looks at how, in the absence of a common doctrine, British Quakers hold together as a faith community, and Chapter 7 examines key aspects of the Quaker way in which diversity is central and essential. Chapter 8 concludes with an exploration of what might define the boundary of British Quakerism; what might hold Friends in all their differences together. This reflects the way we ended each event on the project with an invitation to Friends to continue with that exploration. The challenge here for Friends is to bring real listening and honest speaking to addressing the blocks to "faithful diversity" in their meetings.

The reader should bear in mind throughout that the diversity addressed in this book is the wide range of faith positions and, to a growing extent, personal spiritual practices found today among British Friends. In other ways, Quakers in Britain are far from diverse. In terms of ethnicity, income, occupation and education British Friends are a strikingly homogeneous group. But as this book describes, in their spiritual viewpoints and beliefs British Quakers display a wide range of differences. Yet something clearly does hold Friends in Britain together. In spite of their different spiritual understandings, each Friend recognises something essential in their spirituality that defines them as a Quaker. This book also suggests how these Quaker essentials may have to be articulated in new ways today.

One further point about the theme of this book needs to be made explicit at the outset. While, for reasons Tim and I examine, other faiths are increasingly influencing a significant number of British Friends, the model and the larger part of our discussions here concentrate on the Christian roots of the Religious Society of Friends in relation to more recent developments in British Quakerism. There are two reasons for this emphasis: firstly, Quakerism is historically rooted in the Christian tradition; but secondly, this book is based on the personal experience of its authors. We are both products of a Christian culture, the culture that in very different ways forms the bedrock of each of our spiritual journeys into Quakerism.

Timothy Ashworth

As I write, Alex and I have been working with a group on the same annual Woodbrooke course at which Alex surprised me four years ago with the first version of the diagrams for the model of Quaker diversity he had devised. We started on this occasion by giving the participants a space to consider their own experience of Christian faith and spiritual diversity in their Quaker Meetings. I introduced that first exercise by referring to the difficulty of properly tackling this issue, the inhibition Friends seem to feel about speaking honestly from different faith positions. But I also sketched out a cluster of reasons why this difficulty comes about – which fall into four themes:

1. Religious diversity presents a real intellectual challenge.

The ideas involved in any serious consideration of it are difficult ones. Is it possible to make the claim that your faith is the only true one when we now have so much more awareness of religious diversity? Can any such exclusive truth claim be justified in a time when we are all aware of the part religious identity plays in conflict and violence? Is there a form of religious commitment that does not put limits on tolerance and compassion and openness towards others? How do profound spiritual experiences find expression in ways that communities can celebrate, without increasing the divisions between one community and another?

2. The Quaker context brings its own particular challenges (as would be the case for any religious community).

The community is not a static ideal; it is a messy lived reality. Each Quaker meeting is different. Any reference to what ought to be is framed by each person's experience of what is. Much is at stake. The member of a meeting who opens up any discussion in this territory has to take a risk – of the kind that became vividly clear to Alex and me as we worked with meetings up and down the country. Am I prepared to risk the companionship we have in our meeting (which, while it has limitations, is still precious to me and others) for the possibility of a deeper unity? Opening up areas of difficulty in a meeting can lead to division where people experience hurt, form factions or even leave, making the possibility of deeper community less, not more, attainable.

3. Really understanding each other takes time and effort.

Each of us coming to any such discussion brings the unique experiences of our own faith journeys. When I speak of the significance for me of reading Paul, it will need a real shared commitment on both sides for that to be adequately communicated to Friends who carry the deep conviction that Paul is a misogynist. The Friend for whom involvement in pagan ritual is also part of expressing their spirituality will need to risk some incomprehension as they try to get across to their meeting why and how it is significant and important for them.

4. Some of our experience from our journeys will carry a strong emotional charge.

On the one hand, deep religious or spiritual experiences change or strongly confirm the direction of our lives. On the other, because religion is so bound up with the most positive hopes of human community, when those hopes are betrayed in some serious way, the wounds are deep ones. Our religious experience may be closely linked with formative events from childhood that have played a crucial part in making us who we are and the kinds of relationship we seek or form with others. When deep hurt and religion are tied together, this has consequences for all conversation on religious topics. Whilst healing of such woundedness is possible, this takes real commitment, a sense that such healing is worthwhile and a suitable structure for the process. Unless the healing is thorough, there will be tender spots left in us that may trigger a defensive reaction when someone gets too close.

It is this cluster of challenging issues that has shaped this short book. As Alex and I worked on the project it became clear to us that these different elements cannot be separated; we are not in a position to sort out the intellectual questions concerning spiritual diversity before we give attention to the more personal issues in our communities and in our own lives. They are deeply entangled, and this presents a further need for creating relevant and useful engagement. In writing the following chapters, we respond to the challenge by weaving together elements of our own stories with some of the issues we have witnessed in Quaker meetings, in ways that relate these to particular theological issues. We each also offer the reader insights into some of our personal background to enable them to judge in what ways our discussions in further chapters have been shaped by the more emotionally charged elements of our own life journeys.

In the following pages we invite you to share these journeys with us and to engage with the challenges we identify and explore. We hope you will take what is useful, argue with what is not and informed by your own experience and thoughts contribute with others to this ongoing dialogue.

Chapter 1
Spirit-led diversity

Timothy Ashworth

Dialogue at depth

From the earliest days of working together on the project, participants were invited on the first evening to draw a timeline on which to place key moments in their lives. This invitation included an instruction to indicate times of religious or spiritual change and also to note people and places that were of particular religious or spiritual significance for them. Both Alex and I did one of these whenever we worked with a group, using them as an opportunity to introduce ourselves and give a little of our own backgrounds. Of course, while we varied the way we approached this task, many elements of our individual timelines recurred.

It is important to the purpose of this book that we share these elements of spiritual and religious significance in our personal stories with you, just as it was for participants on our courses to do this kind of sharing with other participants. It gives the hearer or reader a chance to understand how and why a person's present ideas and commitments have arisen and it has the effect of diminishing preconceptions; the labelling of others recedes to be replaced by the interesting complexity of a real individual. In our work with groups this activity became a necessary part of talking with and hearing each other at depth. Here, we offer our stories in the same spirit of engagement with the reader.

From Anglican to Catholic via eastern meditation

I was born in Newmarket in 1954, the son of an Anglican priest and brought up in the Church of England. The eldest of six children, my memories of home are happy ones including those associated with church. From the age of ten I was a choirboy, and while sermons provided a good opportunity to play dice, for the rest of the time I was participating in the worship that characterises Anglican practice and absorbing large quantities of scripture and liturgical language. I am clear that I did not make a personal religious commitment as an adolescent or as a young adult. My father is part of the tolerant middle way in the Anglican Church, genuinely liberal, confident that no emotional pressure, let alone coercion, is appropriate in matters of faith. I was free to find my own way and when I left the church (with the breaking of my voice!) any disappointment of my parents did not engender in me any sort of guilt.

As I look back, I realise that what developed in me from that church upbringing was a sensitivity to an emotional quality of the religious life, a seriousness and indeed a meaningfulness in speaking of the stuff of religion. Religious concerns were not neutral ones to me, but life appeared to be more vital in the world outside the church – an observation that seemed to an adolescent to undermine fundamentally the claims to abundant life made from inside the Christian community.

Having moved away from the church, I eventually found my way to the practice of eastern meditation involving a mantra: the simple repetition of a sound. As my practice deepened, I experienced periods in the meditation where I was discovering a spaciousness and depth which previously I had only glimpsed. And when I came out of meditation, even when it had felt rather unfocused, I noticed that I was able to be more present. I began to participate in groups run by the School of Meditation at its branch in Sheffield and learnt the value both of practising with others and of following some structured teaching to support the meditation.

It was in my early twenties that I reconnected with church. It is still a matter of some wonder to me how I happened to go into St Urban's Catholic Church in Headingley, near where I was living in Leeds, for the 8 o'clock mass. This was after I had worked a nightshift in the local hospital; I was not tired enough to sleep and alternative activities were in short supply at that time on a Sunday. I remember that the reading was about Elijah discovering the still small voice of God, and that the priest spoke of the need to discover stillness in the everyday. I went back a few times before asking the priest if I could come and talk with him. At that stage I had a whole lot of questions, some of which he answered himself. For others he pointed me to things I might read, but these tended to raise a further batch of questions. Engaging with those questions was a very natural and stimulating way of learning. I found myself appreciating the liturgy, including the restless Sunday masses when it appeared that many people would rather have been somewhere else, as well as the weekday masses where there was a stillness and presence that I had not previously discovered in church. I began to identify this quality with the Catholic Church. I could not find it when I revisited the Anglican Church, but it seemed to be a given in the Catholic Church – not something that anyone was making happen. That essential quality was present whether people understood the words of the priest or not, whether they were wholehearted in their worship or not. And I identified it with what I was discovering in meditation: a tangible spacioiusness and depth of presence.

Just over a year after this first visit I was received into the Roman Catholic Church, and a year after that I started studying at Ushaw College near Durham, the seminary for the Catholic dioceses of the north of England. I was ripe for the opportunity for study that it provided. I had felt disengaged from the teaching I received during my school years and had not done well. Now I was in an environment where the questions that concerned me were the focus of the teaching. After two years I was able to pursue a degree at Durham University, where I found that it was the study of scripture that really came alive for me.

A fiery encounter

All through this time, I continued to meditate and for much of it continued to attend my meditation group in Sheffield. While I did have the opportunity to explore points of connection between my meditation practice and my life in the church – Orthodox spirituality and the work of Benedictines in India like Abhishiktananda were the most helpful – for the most part I was happy to live with the intellectual incompatibilities in the teachings of the two traditions. I accepted that they were not resolved in my mind, and I was confident that the means of resolution lay in a deeper immersion into the reality of both traditions rather than a reliance on intellectual insight.

Some eighteen months after I became a priest, I attended a week of teaching by Andrew Cohen, who is best known as the founder of EnlightenNext – the name for both an organisation and a magazine exploring and developing contemporary spirituality. That week in Devon changed my life dramatically. Andrew had an incisive way of questioning. My own dialogues with him were brief but still, twenty years later, stick in the memory. "Which do you value most: to be free or to be a priest?" "To be free" (for what was the gospel that the priesthood served about but to bring people to freedom?). Andrew at one point described enlightenment as an experience of consuming fire. I responded, "Sometimes in prayer or meditation, it feels as if there is a small flame in the heart. How does that small flame become the burning fire you describe?" Andrew replied, "Everything has to go on the flames. You have to surrender 100%: if you surrender 10% you get 10%, 50% you get 50%, but if you surrender 100% ..."

I woke in the middle of the third night at Buckfast Abbey where I was staying and was absolutely clear: I want to surrender everything. This was, after all, the essence of the priesthood. There is the moment before ordination when the priest-to-be lies face down on the floor, a symbol of death before the new life begins. I no longer wanted any compromises.

I have described what happened next so many times. Very soon after making that clear commitment, I experienced a tingling in my chest that rapidly appeared to become hot so that there was a fiery sensation in the central part of my body. It increased moment by moment. It had an element of pain about it but not a pain I wanted to escape, for there was sweetness in it too. And as it happened I felt a change in my consciousness, my awareness of self, of where and how I was observing what went on, which was shifting in a way that I had absolutely no doubt was good. This was everything that I had sought in meditation but overwhelmingly more powerful, beyond anything I had imagined. There seemed nothing I had to do but sustain the sense of assent to what was happening. And once it was established it simply did not stop – not for weeks. While the intense, sharp crackling sensation of the first few hours gradually receded, the feeling I had of burning in the centre of me carried on and on, with variations in intensity.

My world turned upside down

Within six months, I had left the church, was preparing for a postgraduate course at Oxford on the New Testament and its historical context, and I was sharing the role of warden at Aylesbury Quaker Meeting with my wife! Clare and I had known each other at university in Durham and, although we had had little contact in the intervening years, we had kept in touch. Dramatic changes had also been happening for her, and as our paths crossed again we discovered the complementary nature of the journeys we had been on.

At Oxford I was an awkward student, stubborn in my concern to relate the New Testament writings to experience and determined to understand better the experience that underlay the emergence of the Christian movement. At Aylesbury Quaker Meeting, I began to appreciate the honesty and directness of some of the older Friends and felt a deep connection with meeting for worship, whether the Sunday meeting or the meeting for business. Listening for guidance, for the living word, had always been an important part of my prayer life, but now, after the experience in Devon, it was central to how I was seeking to live. Only towards the end of this period at Aylesbury Meeting while I studied at Oxford did the question of membership of the Society of Friends become a real possibility; at one meeting I stood and asked for the support of Friends as Clare and I sought clarity on this, but we decided it was not right for us then to make that step.

My time at Oxford was extraordinarily stimulating and fruitful, allowing me to explore what I had gone through in relation to the Bible and the Christian tradition. However, my approach did not fit easily into established academic channels and I had to move on. Still doing work on the Bible, I applied for an advertised teaching post at Woodbrooke Quaker Study Centre. Preparing for this assessment process, which involved a presentation as well as interviews, was the first time I had studied Quakerism, both the early movement and Friends today. I used Aylesbury Meeting library and also went up to Friends House in London; I bought various books and spent some time in the library there. I still remember the excitement of reading Douglas Gwyn's *Apocalypse of the Word*. So much resonated with my own experience of a couple of years earlier and also with what I believed I was discovering about early Christian experience: of being guided; of light thrown upon the nature of sin and liberation from it; of changes in sense perception as people went through transformation. I recognised the way their direct experience diminished the need for traditional forms of worship and signalled the end of the centrality of a liturgical calendar; how anticipation of an imminent end to life as it had been known was linked with their sense of being on the threshold of a glorious new beginning, and with a vivid awareness of the collective nature of transformation.

I incorporated these ideas into my presentation on the weekend of the Woodbrooke interview and then subsequently in my teaching, seeking to reveal the parallels between early Christian and early Quaker experience.

Beyond healing

Ever since that first presentation, I have been aware of real difficulties that many Friends have with the Christian story – both its roots in scripture and also its subsequent expression in the church. For a good number of people, the Society of Friends has provided a community with genuine religious seriousness but with a high degree of individual freedom, often in direct and welcome contrast to previous experiences of church. So I referred in my presentation to the value of each person looking at the difficulties they have with scripture and the Christian tradition, not to deny or belittle those difficulties but to acknowledge their existence and how they might limit an appreciation of what is actually present and worthwhile for Friends today.

Alex was at Woodbrooke in my second term and joined the course that I ran. I could tell he had a real problem with aspects of what I was offering, but at that stage we were not thinking or talking about future work together. It was a while later that we shared our feeling that there was not just a need for Friends to acknowledge the difficulties some had with the Christian tradition but a need for actual healing. Drawing on a programme developed by the Unitarian Church called "Healing our Religious Past", Alex and I put together a four-day course, which we intended to be spacious enough to allow participants to work on those things they knew were sources of present pain or limitation. The event was a powerful one. Several participants noted real benefits in confronting some of their past hurts. What also proved valuable was a collective fruit of the work: having experienced a measure of release from old ways of considering the tradition, new questions and new ways of engaging with the Christian story started to surface. Time was limited so what we managed was only a beginning, but there was a real excitement among the participants about tackling the question: if the Christian story is not what I thought it was, what then is it, and where is the life in it now?

A couple of weeks after the course, I rang Alex to talk with him about my sense that there was a major piece of work to be done in this area. He had also been thinking about the course and its impact, and we were in agreement that we should do more thinking on this to see what was needed and what we could offer. We explored the possibility of us both working on this project full-time over a limited period, with the aim of seeing if we could really help things change in the Yearly Meeting. It took some time to get to the two-weekend form offered as part of Woodbrooke's off-site work that finally emerged. This form was less ambitious in scale than our original idea but capable of being sustained over a period of several years, which is what happened.

Do I belong or not?

I went into this work as an attender rather than member of the Society of Friends. Over the time of the project and since, my Quaker life has very much revolved around Woodbrooke and my involvement with my local meeting has been limited, although during this time my eldest son sought and was accepted into membership in his own right when he was fourteen. I was always deeply aware of Alex's involvement in his own local meeting, area meeting (then called monthly meeting) and the Yearly Meeting, so where precisely was my interest in the project?

One dimension of the answer is simply in connection with my own work at Woodbrooke. As Biblical Studies Tutor my work is directly affected by the difficulties the project sought to address. But there is a further dimension. It is rare that on any course I am running I do not have the decision to make when I am talking with a group of Friends as to whether I speak of the Society of Friends in the first or third person. I never find myself saying you, thus separating myself from the group. I regularly slip into saying we. This wavering genuinely reflects my position.

I know of no other community where the experience that I have described makes better sense. I was grabbed by the collar and lifted out of the church and yet the very experience that separated me from the church joined me in new and powerful ways to the Christian tradition. That seems to me exactly where early Friends were and where Friends in Britain have been for much of their existence.

Along with that fact, there is the actual experience of worshipping and learning and teaching with Friends. Regularly, and certainly in the life of the project, there have been moments together with Friends of great openness where perceptions appeared to be shifting – not so much in the production of new ideas, but rather towards a greater confidence in a holding and nurturing presence beyond words and structure.

Yet engagement with Friends can sometimes lead me to feel at a distance. Just occasionally I encounter flippant, even mocking, portrayals of the Christian tradition. "Surely we have all moved on from this," I hear, "You cannot take all the traditional Christian stuff seriously." This is particularly difficult to respond to as the seriousness and respect that would make some real dialogue possible is not present. Also difficult is a not uncommonly heard view that "while I truly respect those for whom the Christian tradition matters, it is not of importance to me." This view seems to allow space for the one for whom it does matter, but that space is only apparent. My Christian faith carries within it a vision of unity. When I hear such a line, I know for certain we are not sharing the same vision of what unity might be. And that is not to assume that the only vision of unity possible is a Christian one. The key question it raises is this: how can we share real unity if there is no interest in, or at least an openness to understand, something so central to my faith? Having experienced the depth of unity in a more traditional Christian environment, I do not believe leaving that was a call to accept a less vibrant and integrated community. If it was a true call, it can only have been to greater depth, something that might indeed embrace greater diversity but from a solidly established experience of unity. A world-changing community of faith is unlikely to be sustained on the basis of the lowest common denominator of what we can all agree on.

Spirit-led diversity – an opportunity, a responsibility

For a long time, the project did not fundamentally change my position in relation to membership. As I have said, those moments of real depth and life that drew me in were countered by other moments where the difficulty of getting beyond a superficial understanding and engagement with the Christian tradition distanced me. But the morning after Alex first presented his model to a group at Woodbrooke, I woke up feeling unmistakably challenged over membership. Why was that? Well, it should be apparent from all I have said that I believe I have been led into this involvement with Friends, from my perspective, led by God. While I have heard Alex many times describe his own sense of being led among Friends, I do not think I had put those two positions together in a way that appropriately challenged me. Through his model, Alex had found a way of picturing how Friends hold different positions in relation to the Christian tradition – some right within it, others standing clearly apart from it – and how this diversity has come about. For the first time, my sense of Friends in all their diversity belonging together in the same community was combined with the affirmation that this whole situation is "God-led".

Once I had thought of Quaker diversity in these terms, there came with it a sense of the demands that are laid upon all Friends as a consequence. Specifically, it rules out any caricature of the position of the other. It cannot be OK to mock the faith position of another – Christian or non-Christian; it cannot be OK to regard a person on the other side of the community to you – whether Christian or non-Christian – as not a true Quaker. It is not uncommon to encounter the view that only the Christian Quaker is the real thing or, conversely, that a true Quaker is one who has left behind traditional Christianity. Putting this rejection of caricature in positive terms, the coexistence of significant diversity within the same God-led community lays on each of us the commitment to seek honestly to understand the position of the other in all its real difference, which includes, when necessary, asking difficult questions. This was one of our regular instructions on the project: to really hear what someone is saying and not be too quick to translate it into your own terms, your own form of words. This means taking seriously the idea that the differences may well be genuine and not simply the result of defining or describing things differently. It is just such a commitment to honesty that keeps me in the slightly uncomfortable position of straddling the worlds of both Friends and church. To return to full membership of the church or to enter membership of Friends both seem options that are less honest than being an attender at each.

Is this demanding dialogue not just another version of the call to be truthful? I see it as an affirmation that real community comes about where there is honest sharing, where the barriers are down and people are together in a place of authentic openness and listening. Throughout our work on the project we did not lose sight of an essential linkage between Friends' depth of engagement with each other and Quaker social action – which has traditionally sprung from and been supported by this practice. It is important to remember what extraordinary possibilities arise from time spent together in such a place of real inspiration. Friends have generations of experience of seeking this space when they gather for worship or decision-making. Faithful witness of Friends in the past has bequeathed to Quakers today a firm structure that is nonetheless open to movements of the Spirit, to an awareness that in real communication at depth there is the potential for radical change.

It is quite possible that the kind of dialogue described above is happening nowhere else and that this is a distinctive calling for the Quaker community. There are of course other settings where dialogue is taking place across religious and philosophical dividing lines, but what is distinctive about Friends is that the real engagement between Christians, or those with Christian leanings, and people who in their religious/spiritual lives identify themselves in a whole variety of other ways is happening within the same community of faith. Each person may be engaging with what would normally be seen as fundamentally different understandings of the religious life, but each with a sense – itself articulated in different ways – of being led by God to live and worship and celebrate in the one Quaker community.

Chapter 2

Surfing the sea of faith

Alex Wildwood

Throughout our work on the project it was clear that authentic dialogue, of the kind we were advocating, requires a commitment to disciplined listening as Friends explore their faith with one another. Tim and I sought to illustrate this commitment whenever we worked with groups by inviting participants to eavesdrop on our own continuing conversation. In their evaluations afterwards many Friends mentioned how valuable they had found this, appreciating particularly the care with which we talked and listened to one another. Conversing in this way, with the group listening in, enabled us to raise difficult issues and get to deeper questions in an authentic way.

Essential to this process were the real respect that came from working together and sharing a conscious intention to be in dialogue, a willingness to make ourselves vulnerable – to admit our uncertainties and to be open to new light in the ministry of the other, and a commitment to neither avoid nor make light of the real differences between us. We were never out to score points, we did not take up positions as Christian versus non-Christian, nor did we attempt to persuade the other of our point of view. We simply sought to understand and appreciate the other's faith experience whilst remaining true to our own. What became clear from this process – and apparent every time we shared our timelines – was just how different our spiritual experiences and identities were.

My early life experience
I did not grow up in a religious family. My father was an agnostic and my mother an occasional church attender who sought confirmation in the Presbyterian Church when I was eleven years

old. Although I had been baptised as a baby, this was more a matter of social convention than a statement of religious intent. Apart from attending church every now and then to keep my mother company, I mainly encountered Christianity through the schools I attended. In assemblies and classes for religious instruction, and through compulsory chapel attendance every Sunday when I was at boarding school, I was exposed to a religious tradition that, from the start, I found both disturbing and incomprehensible.

But then in general my memories of childhood are not happy ones; I recall my family as materially secure but not close. Sent away to boarding school at thirteen, I felt alone and unhappy much of the time. I learnt to hide what I was feeling, and in my isolation I patched together my own eclectic system of meaning, my own philosophy of life. The product of an educational system that prized rationality above all else, I learnt to be habitually sceptical. Spiritually, I developed a defensive self-reliance; I was never a joiner and grew up without any meaningful affinity or allegiance to any larger body, whether school, church or nation. My great consolation came from being in nature. Fascinated by the variety and forms of animals and plants, it was in the natural world that I encountered a sense of the numinous. In nature I felt an awesome, mysterious power at work. Losing myself in the observation and study of nature, I spent my schooldays intending to become a naturalist.

In contrast to these private spiritual stirrings, my childhood contact with Christianity was bleak. I came to associate the word "Christian" with unthinking adherence to impossible beliefs and a view of the world that flew in the face of reason. I learnt that the Christian story had to be accepted as literally true and that it was a Christian duty to impose one's beliefs on others – an attitude I found arrogant, and still do. The bodily-sense of Christianity I carry from childhood is of a religion of shoulds and oughts, a prescriptive faith morbidly obsessed with sacrifice and suffering. To my young imagination, there was no way that the barbarity of Jesus' death could be mitigated through being understood as a sacred mystery. Given this poor introduction, it is hardly surprising that on my timeline I drew my early encounters with Christianity as a stark, forbidding Cross throwing a long dark shadow over my formative years. On an emotional level I have been in negative reaction to this childhood indoctrination most of my adult life. I still feel put off by a tradition I perceive as weighed down by centuries of doctrinal assertions with which even the most casual enquirer is obliged to engage. (And this is before taking into account the violence perpetrated in Christianity's name or the hypocrisy and double standards of some of its supposedly most ardent practitioners.)

So I can readily identify with those Friends who have distanced themselves from the Christianity of their upbringing, or who regard Christian faith as belonging to a bygone age – as the majority of the population in Britain now do. I still frequently find myself triggered by Christian imagery and language and generally avoid ecumenical church services for this reason. However, being in dialogue with Tim has taught me to make an effort to check whether I have actually heard the intention in a (Christian) speaker's words and am not simply reacting to what the words or phrases have restimulated in me.

But I also recognise in my reactivity a real loss, an impoverishment of my own spiritual life. Because of negative associations with being subjected to scripture in a totally unimaginative and dogmatic way at school, the Bible has remained, literally, a closed book for me. I even find myself unable to read any text peppered with biblical references because I have learnt to associate these with rote learning, with an imposed orthodoxy and with point-scoring or proving someone wrong. Scripture, sadly, evokes painful memories of being bored and lectured at.

So I recognise in myself the tendency Tim speaks of when he describes the way British Friends can be hurtfully dismissive of what they assume he means by his Christian faith, or are merely tolerant of what he holds most dear. Discussing my early experience of the Christian tradition with Tim I observed that I seemed to have picked up all of the guilt and none of the glory of Christian faith.

A child of the sixties

Not surprisingly in the light of these early experiences, when I left school in 1968 and went to college I became a militant atheist. This was the time of student sit-ins, of protests against the Vietnam war and radical critiques of the military-industrial complex. We were a privileged generation, enjoying the benefits of post-war affluence and higher education, but also increasingly aware of the cost of that privilege to others around the world. I got involved in Marxist politics; revolution was the way to a better world. The 1960s also saw the launch of the global environmental movement with the publication of Rachel Carson's groundbreaking *Silent Spring* in 1962 and the founding of Greenpeace to protest against nuclear tests in the Pacific – and later to "Save the Whales". There was a widespread mood of both rebelliousness and experimentation, of rejection of the old order and a growing desire to know things experientially. Even established institutions seemed to be embracing this questioning spirit. When Pope John XXIII summoned the Second Vatican Council in 1962, its express purpose was "to open the windows and let in the fresh air of change".

As an undergraduate living away from home for the first time, I certainly felt liberated from the old, oppressive religious forms I had grown up with. Like so many others, I was able to enjoy a newfound openness and freedom to explore spiritual realities in a new way. Eastern faith traditions were becoming more widely talked about and recreational drugs were seen as a legitimate way of expanding consciousness. It was an exciting, challenging time to be alive.

Women, Earth and Spirit

When I first married in the early 1970s the wedding took place in a Register Office. Our ceremony was a purely secular affair; we felt no need for religious rites of any kind. It was simply a legal agreement between two people, witnessed by their families. When my first child was born at home a few years later I was there at his birth. Being present at that raw edge between life and death, faced with the immediacy and uncertainty of existence, I found myself awakened to a tremendous sense of wonder. But my awe was as much at the capacities and resilience of the female body as of anything transcendent. I still felt no need of "God", even at this most profoundly life-changing moment.

But during the 1970s I experienced a subtle change in outlook. Partly through being present at my son's birth and partly through his mother's involvement in the women's movement, I became aware of how women perceived and related to the world very differently from the way I did. For the first time I heard women speak of "the Goddess" – a new language for the divine that resonated in me. A few years later in the early 1980s I was going through the trauma of divorce and separation from my son. I sought counselling but also felt hungry for more, for something overtly spiritual.

In ways I do not consciously remember, my yearning for community and connection (combined with both my childhood experience of the numinous in nature and my growing ecological awareness) led me to the company of feminist-inspired pagans. Here I found myself in groups of women, plus a few men, who marked the seasons of the year in festivals created to celebrate the Earth's abundance and honour "Her" vitality. In this primal, sensual kind of religion my scepticism was somehow sidestepped. I learnt to honour cycles of death and rebirth, to recognise the need for times to sow, to harvest and to lie fallow. Women taught me to respect and value the darkness as well as the light. As religious observances related to the seasons and to the land, these pagan practices felt especially meaningful to me. They engaged parts of me the Christianity of my childhood had either ignored or condemned – the Earthly, the bodily, the intuitive and the feminine.

I also discovered I could appreciate and enjoy ritual when it was created out of the life experience of the participants themselves, when it arose from the needs and creativity of a worshipping group. In these pagan gatherings we enjoyed experimenting with new forms, working spontaneously with the energy of the moment and discovering our own authority. Worshipping generally in the open air and often at those liminal times of dusk or dawn, we opened ourselves to spiritual powers beyond, within and all around us. We sought to experience our connectedness to the Earth, our belonging to the physical, sensual world, and our embeddedness in the sacred web of life.

Awakening to "our deep ecology"

By the late 1980s I was working in television, and while researching a programme on people's responses to the threat of nuclear war I came across the work of Chellis Glendinning, an American psychologist and political activist who was offering workshops on "Telling our Nuclear Stories". She had discovered that inviting people to talk about how they first became aware of weapons of mass destruction was a powerful way of breaking through the apathy and denial that many of us understandably felt in the face of possible annihilation. It was through her work that I came into contact with Buddhist scholar and ecological activist Joanna Macy.

Joanna ran what were initially called Despair and Empowerment workshops[1]. With colleagues she devised a series of practices to help people face their heartfelt responses to the growing threats to our world. By allowing themselves to feel this pain – whether as grief, rage, numbness or despair – people awakened their compassion and realised experientially their interconnectedness with the rest of life. By creating safe spaces where people could share their concerns for the world at the deepest level, these practices enabled people to break through their "psychic numbing", their feeling of being overwhelmed by the suffering of our world.

Participating in Joanna's workshops awoke me to an immediate awareness (rather than an intellectual understanding) that, as rainforest activist John Seed puts it, "we are the rocks dancing". I absorbed the Buddhist view that the physical, material world is our greater Self, and that working for justice and peace, or taking action for threatened species and habitats, is spiritually an act of Self-preservation. I soon became engrossed in this pioneering emotional activism in which elements of politics, therapy and spiritual practice are skilfully combined. Through my involvement I was also introduced to the Tibetan form of Mahayana Buddhism and to the mindfulness practices of Zen monk and peace activist Thich Nhat Hanh.

In Joanna I met for the first time someone who embodied a truly prophetic voice, someone who "told it like it was" and who, in her international advocacy work, was clearly speaking truth to power. Joanna encouraged those she worked with not to be afraid of our deep caring for the world, to realise that "the heart that breaks is the heart that can contain the world." She spoke of the need in this time to "sustain the gaze". She taught us that daring to face our almost unbearable pain at the destruction of the world was to choose to be conscious, to refuse the distractions

1 The work Joanna Macy initiated later became known as "deep ecology work" and is now known as "The Work That Reconnects".

our culture so seductively fosters and on which the destructive addiction of consumerism depends.

Led amongst Friends

At this stage of my life, in my late thirties, I went to live in an intentional community in East London that had been established originally by Quakers as an experiment in all-age communal living. (This was my second encounter with Friends. The first was when I attended what was, in effect, the junior school to Leighton Park, the Quaker secondary school near Reading.) It was through living in this community and through co-counselling that I met my present wife. Seren had been a Friend since her teens and seemed to have no difficulty weaving together her own feminist, pagan and Quaker spiritualities. Other than Seren, the first Quakers I spent much time with were the community residents and the activists who visited from time to time. I remember us giving parking space to the Quaker Peace Action Caravan and meeting an activist heavily involved in Cruise-Watch who drove through the night following convoys of nuclear weapons being moved furtively by road around the country. One member moved into the community having been diagnosed with a terminal cancer, and when she died I attended a Quaker memorial meeting for the first time. I was struck by the truthfulness of the ministry especially when, after much praise for the dear departed, someone from the community agreed how lovely she was but added that she could be a real pain to live with.

With the benefit of hindsight I can now see that in being drawn to Friends (even though I was not yet worshipping with them) I was gradually coming to accept that culturally I am thoroughly Christian, that, albeit unconsciously, the imagery and symbols of Christianity have played an important, subliminal role in my spiritual formation. Even in my reactivity to what early Friends would have called the empty forms of church religion as I had first encountered it, there was a part of me that wanted to find honest accommodation with the religious heritage of my birth, that sensed there might be something richer there. Living where I was and being impressed by the Quakers I was meeting, the Religious Society of Friends seemed an obvious place to start this exploration.

When I moved out of London and set up household with

Seren in Shropshire, we started to attend meeting for worship together. I read avidly about Quakers, trying to understand the basis of Friends' worship and witness. What I experienced with Friends was a remarkable attitude of real tolerance; I discovered in the meeting community a place where people were encouraged to discover faith for themselves, at their own pace and, to a great extent, in their own way. But whilst I personally benefited greatly from this culture of acceptance (carrying as I did a lot of self-judgement), I was also drawn to Quakers because they embodied a history of finding unity, of being led to act collectively for peace and justice as a faith community. Their track record of social witness knocked spots off the alternative spiritual paths I had been exploring. And in an era when Margaret Thatcher pronounced that there was "no such thing as society", Quakers seemed to offer an inspiring counter-balance to the extreme individualism of the age.

Here was a faith community that had done away with so much of what I found abhorrent in the Christianity of my childhood. These were people who believed that illumination was available to ordinary women and men simply by sitting still, letting go of personal wants and preferences and listening together for guidance by the Spirit in the expectant waiting of meeting for worship. It helped that many of the Quakers I met were encouragingly eccentric individuals strongly committed to the practical relief of suffering in this world, rather than theological speculation about some heavenly realm to come. And the lack of emphasis on doctrine amongst Quakers, their refusal to make correct belief the basis of faith, together with the absence of outward symbols of Christian faith in meeting houses, all made this a safe place for me to explore more mainstream religion.

Whilst others have spoken of an experience of coming home when they first attended meeting for worship, for me the feeling of belonging has happened more gradually. But from the start, being part of this community felt intensely right to me. With hindsight I would say I felt led amongst Friends; I had a strong feeling that I was meant to be here, that something (I could not have explained what) had been nudging me, quite forcefully, towards this community. I made the commitment of membership less than a year after I first started attending meeting on a regular basis. Interestingly, at no point did anyone challenge my

prior beliefs or suggest I renounce my previous spiritual practices – and nor did I feel obliged to do so. I have continued to
feel more in tune with the pagan cycle of the year than with the
festivals of the church calendar.

Honouring my spiritual ancestry

Given both my continuing aversion to doctrinal Christianity and
the varied spiritual influences in my life I have been describing,
participants on our project events were often surprised to find
churches featuring as landmarks on the timeline I drew as part
of the opening evening's activities. One was a church that fea-
tured in a significant sequence of events in the late 1980s, after
I had met Seren but before we were married. We were both at
one of Joanna Macy's workshops near Bath when during a break
in the programme Seren said there was somewhere nearby she
wanted to take me. This turned out to be the Saxon chapel at
Bradford-on-Avon, a building that was decommissioned as a
church and used for centuries as a wool-store – thus retaining
the stark simplicity of its original design and purpose. We arrived
at dusk, pleasantly surprised to find the building open. Unable
to find any lighting, I was feeling my way around the walls when
I suddenly found myself on my knees and a voice (audible only
to me, internally) told me, "You have to respect what people
have honoured in these places." Without speaking, I went over
and sat quietly beside Seren in the darkness and was then given
an image of a couple getting married in a small country church
decked in flowers. As we left the building I said to her: "I think
we have to get married." She said it was the most unromantic
proposal imaginable!

But so it was that, even though we were both Friends attending our local meeting, eighteen months later we were married in
just such a country church, in a ceremony led by a vicar we had
become friends with through an ecumenical study group, where
we were studying Matthew Fox's *Original Blessing*. Our wedding
witnesses included family and Friends from our local meeting;
the reading we chose was the biblical call to a life of trust: Jesus'
injunction to his disciples, "Consider the lilies of the field", a
call not to worry about tomorrow or the means of our material
survival. A friend played the didgeridoo, providing an appropri-

ate lamentation for both the aboriginal peoples of the world and the vanishing species of the Earth. True to my "vision" we had decked the Lady Chapel in garlands of greenery. This time when I married, the numinous, the Sacred Mystery, was central to the proceedings.

Although attending church services is still too evocative of painful childhood memories for me – our wedding being the exception – I have continued to have powerful experiences in church buildings throughout my adult life, especially when visiting churches or cathedrals quietly on my own, seeking sanctuary from the busyness of the outside world. But then, this apparent anomaly is not really so surprising. Even for those of us who are not believers, churches are still the cultural repositories of our collective honouring of the sacred. They literally enshrine the spiritual aspirations of our predecessors. And sometimes I visit them simply because I feel in need of something more than I find in the plainness of a Friends meeting house.

A power greater than ourselves

When I had already made my commitment to the Quaker community, a further significant influence on my spiritual journey was my involvement in Twelve Step fellowships for recovery from addiction/compulsion. Here I found a companionship I have sometimes felt lacking among Friends, a fellowship and community that is born of people admitting their own poverty of spirit and realising they are not in control of their lives. Earlier generations of Friends were clear they could achieve little in their own strength; today Quakers seem to struggle more with accepting their dependence on "God" (my use of inverted commas epitomises the dilemma).

What I have found so valuable in Twelve Step fellowships has been the honesty of admitting to each other the times and ways we have fallen short (the literal meaning of sin). In recovery fellowships there is no shaming or blaming; people listen to one another without offering advice, trying to fix each other or proffering psychological explanations that offer premature forgiveness. The welcoming acceptance is similar to what I find with Friends, but paradoxically I have generally experienced a stronger experience of faith in Twelve Step meetings as people

share their stories, warts and all. Accepting their personal brokenness and their powerlessness over destructive habits, the
lives of recovering addicts attest to everyday miracles of personal
transformation.

In the Twelve Steps the second step speaks of how, as people who accept that we are powerless over our addictions and
attachments, we "came to believe in a power greater than ourselves" that could restore us to sanity/wholeness. I really warm to
the pragmatism of this theology. As with Quakerism, it does not
assume people have to start by believing something, nor does
it impose an orthodoxy of what that greater power might be.
Individuals are encouraged to discover how they experience it
for themselves. Newcomers who may be put off by the word God
(often because of previous encounters with dogmatic faiths) are
invited to let their greater power be the group itself, or to imagine it as the power of love at work in their lives. Whenever the
word God is used in the written versions of the Twelve Steps it
is qualified as "God as we understand God". What is most significant is not that we are sharing a common understanding or
orthodoxy, but choosing to turn our lives over to a source of
guidance beyond ourselves.

In both the Twelve Steps and the Quaker way, the common
commitment is to the surrendered life. The simplest account I
have heard of Quakerism is from British Friend Carole Hamby
who described it as "a life lived under guidance". I remember
one Sunday morning visiting the historic meeting house at Bewd-
ley and having an experience of a truly gathered meeting that
touched me deeply. In the quiet of that plain, seventeenth century room, amplified somehow by the faithfulness of generations
of Friends worshipping there, something tangible pervaded the
stillness. Had I asked those Friends present about it afterwards
they might have interpreted this sense of presence variously as
the power of love, the spirit of community, the intention to act
for good, or they might have been quite happy to speak of it
as God or Christ. For me, what we shared, what gathered us in
worship, was an experience of something beyond our everyday
selves, "whose" presence can be known to us when we quieten
what contemporary mystic Eckhart Tolle calls "the egoic mind".

34

Facing a dilemma

I started attending meeting partly because of the openness and acceptance I found in the Religious Society of Friends and partly because it did not remind me too much of the Christianity of my childhood. But the more involved I became the more I appreciated the extent to which Quaker faith was rooted in Christianity. Realising this poses a dilemma for me. How can my clear sense of being led amongst Friends be reconciled with being unable to call myself any kind of Christian? Do I really belong here or is the Society (in its very tolerance) merely a comfortable resting place for me? I can sometimes feel like a brash newcomer arriving among Friends confident that I know what the Society ought to be and how it needs to change – without having the humility to discover what it has been and is essentially about. Perhaps I want it to conform to my needs rather than risk exposing myself to its potentially transforming message. The image comes to mind of a visitor, welcomed into someone's house, who immediately sets about re-arranging the furniture to their own taste and liking!

Paradoxically, it is my very sympathy with the Quaker commitment to truth that leads me to question whether newcomers such as myself may not be subtly or blatantly distorting the traditional ways of Friends. Might we be threatening the very integrity of Quaker worship and witness? In facing the challenge of this question I realised I needed to find (for myself in the first instance) a way of understanding how Friends became so diverse, and how the different strands of Quakerism might relate to one another with integrity. When the project ended I turned my attention to this problem, and it was out of these deliberations that the model I describe in the next chapter emerged.

Chapter 3

Mapping our diversity: "the whole banana"

Alex Wildwood

The model I introduce in this chapter is expressed as a series of simple diagrams illustrating key stages in the evolving relationship of British Quakers to the Christian tradition over the last 350 years. It was originally devised for use with participants on courses and events that Tim and I ran, to help explain the origins and development of the current spiritual diversity of British Friends. An adapted version of the model designed for a readership is offered here with the same purpose in mind – as a tool for opening up discussion. We hope it might help Friends of diverse views and approaches to Quaker faith to engage in a process of honest dialogue and find ways of talking more deeply about their faith with one another.

My own understanding of Quakerism was deepened immeasurably by being able to spend a whole year as a student at Woodbrooke Quaker Study Centre, when there was still a term-time programme and a strong sense of a residential community. As well as the stimulation of input from Woodbrooke tutors, I had the great privilege of meeting Quakers from different yearly meetings, which really helped me appreciate where the theologically liberal Quakerism of Britain Yearly Meeting fits in the overall picture of the faith and practice of Friends worldwide. During my time at Woodbrooke I took the opportunity of immersing myself in Quaker history and spirituality. This grounding in Quaker history especially helped me formulate the model, and is the essential context in which I explain it here.

Quaker Christianity

Quakers as a worshipping community came into existence during the English Civil War, a time of tremendous turmoil when political structures and religious orthodoxies were both being challenged. For a brief period, all kinds of alternatives to the established order seemed possible. Contemporary accounts make clear that people saw the hand of God at work in these upheavals, and the expectation that God's kingdom would soon be established upon the Earth was widespread. The first Quakers emerged from this context of social, political and religious ferment with a particular understanding of how God's kingdom was coming among them, directing all their activities and bringing about a community that could transform the world. Their success in the early days was extraordinary, and further confirmed for them their conviction that they were in the vanguard of God's work to bring about a world of justice and peaceful co-existence. But their challenge to established patterns of power, authority and custom meant that this early success led to them being persecuted and to severe legal sanctions being taken against them.

Such repression by the state reflected just how radical the message of the early Quakers was and the threat it posed to the established order. These "Friends in the Truth" asserted a distinctive experience of Christian revelation: their understanding of the Second Coming – that Christ had come to teach his people himself – meant they experienced the risen Christ as a living presence amongst them. This conviction led early Friends to challenge the religious order of their day and to advocate both a completely different kind of worship and a radically alternative form of church government. Through the lens of history, Quakers are seen as a non-conformist group within the Protestant Reformation, but that is not how early Friends regarded themselves or understood their calling. Rather, they believed the means by which religious factions would all be brought to an end had been revealed to them, and God's will could now guide both government and individuals directly. This immediate divine guidance, Friends claimed, could now be known in the hearts of ordinary men and women without the need for any intermediary – whether priest, scripture or religious rite.

Although early Quakers were prophesying the end of institutional religion, their basic theological frame of reference and

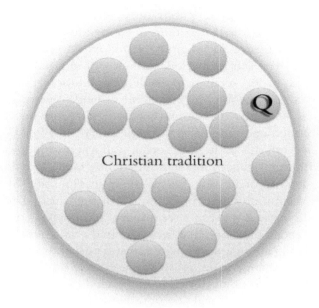

Diagram 1: The Quaker community as one group
among other Christian sects and denominations

their own religious language and symbolism were unmistakably
Christian. The Quaker way of life and worship had been revealed
to them as the true embodiment of Christian faith; it was, in William Penn's phrase, "primitive Christianity revived"[1]. So for most
of its history the Quaker movement has been clearly identified,
from within and from outside the Religious Society of Friends, as
a Christian body. To all the generations of British Friends prior
to the mid-twentieth century, the Inward Light that illuminates
and guides each individual *was* the Light of Christ (and this
remains so for the majority of Friends worldwide today). The

1 The title of his tract of 1696, quoted on pp.102–03.
2 For a concise history of Quakerism, see Pink Dandelion, *The Quakers: A very short introduction* (Oxford: Oxford University Press, 2008),
pp.19–36. For an even shorter, six page outline of the historical stages
in Britain, see his "A brief history of British Quakerism" in *Who We Are:
Questions of Quaker identity, Booklet A: Our Tradition and Today* (London:
Quaker Home Service and Woodbrooke, 1995), pp.8–14.

first diagram of the model therefore shows Quakers historically embedded within this larger body, the Christian tradition as a whole. It illustrates the era, lasting almost 300 years, of what can be described as Quaker-Christianity[2].

In Diagram 1, I locate Quakers clearly within the Christian tradition, but near the perimeter to indicate a paradox at the heart of Quaker spirituality. While basing their faith firmly on the example and teachings of Jesus and on their understanding of the early Christian church, Quaker practices and the language they used also expressed their sense of being called to move beyond religious forms, that is, beyond doctrinal faith to an immediate experience of divine guidance. Reflecting these two dimensions of Quaker faith, Friends developed a consciously inclusive terminology. So from the earliest days, Friends used metaphors such as "the Inward Light", "the Seed", "the Inward Guide" or "the Inward Teacher" – phrases that suggested the universal nature of the direct, unmediated divine guidance on which they individually and collectively depended.

An illuminating example of how Quakers embraced this paradox is found in the writings of Francis Howgill, one of the group of early Quaker ministers known as the Valiant Sixty who travelled around the country spreading the message of Friends in the early decades of the Quaker movement:

Why may not the Heathen have the Light of the Spirit? … The grace of God hath appeared unto all men. And who art thou that makes exceptions? Though the Heathen do not know Christ of the Spirit by the name of Christ and Spirit, … they have the thing … and I say, Nay, these men were not born without Light … God is rich unto all." [3]

These universalist understandings of early Friends, being so far beyond the orthodoxy of the day, were one of the reasons why many of their contemporaries questioned whether Quakers were

3 Francis Howgill, *Francis Howgill's Testimony concerning Edward Burrough*, in Edward Burrough, *The Memorable Works of a Son of Thunder and Consolation*, 1672, quoted in Jeni Edwards, *The New Age and the Church* (Youlgrave, Derbyshire: Bumblebee Booklets, 1992). William Penn and John Woolman expressed views that have been seen as similarly universalist in two better-known sayings: see *Quaker Faith & Practice* 19.28 and 26.61, respectively.

really Christians at all. For their part, Quakers continued to challenge what they saw as the apostasy of the church, its abandoning
of true, experiential, Christian faith. The extremely bold claim
Quakers made for immediate divine guidance resulted in them
being prosecuted and persecuted for their heretical beliefs.

Even such a brief glance at early Quaker history reveals how
embedded Quaker origins are in the Christian tradition. While
challenging the established church, and being shunned by it,
early Friends drew their theology and their inspiration directly
and exclusively from the Christian source. They were not just
planted in Christian soil, but deeply and ineradicably rooted in
its prophetic heritage. With these firm Christian roots, and having once seen themselves as the promoters of the true expression of Christian faith, how have British Quakers today come to
represent such a broad spectrum of beliefs and spiritual practices – some having little or no connection with Christianity? The
answer can be seen to lie mainly in the influence of two historical
developments: one internal to the Yearly Meeting and one a matter of the external cultural context.

The influence of liberal "Quakerism"

In the nineteenth century, London Yearly Meeting – as Quakers
in Britain were then corporately known – witnessed the interplay
of two opposing theological forces. During the 1830s and 1840s
there was a strong evangelical revival that sought to pull British
Friends more towards the mainstream of Christian faith. Then,
towards the end of the century, Friends of a more liberal persuasion argued that the Yearly Meeting should take heed of contemporary developments such as Biblical criticism and new scientific
discoveries and theories.

Diagram 2 of the model illustrates the tension between these
two historical forces within the Yearly Meeting. It shows the evangelical revival seeking to move Friends more towards mainstream
Christianity, in opposition to the liberal Quaker emphasis on
direct, unmediated faith, which kept Friends at the periphery of
the Christian tradition. But at this historical juncture Friends were
nevertheless united in seeing themselves as a Christian body.

Then in the late nineteenth century, the modernisers within
the Yearly Meeting were active in setting up the Manchester Con-
ference of London Yearly Meeting in 1895, a key event that led to

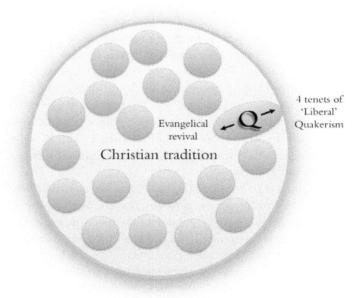

Diagram 2: British Quakers pulled in opposite
directions during the nineteenth century

liberal theology subsequently becoming the dominant influence
in the Yearly Meeting. Significantly, it was only at this point that
the word "Quakerism" appeared, suggesting something distinct
and autonomous within the larger framework of Christianity.
Central to an understanding of subsequent developments are
the four tenets of theologically liberal Quakerism, identified by
Ben Pink Dandelion, Professor of Quaker Studies at Birmingham
University, which became prominent in London Yearly Meeting
in those closing decades of the nineteenth century[4].

The first tenet of liberal Quakerism is the belief that faith
must be rooted in experience; that experience, not scripture,
should be primary. Whilst an emphasis on experiential faith
can be found throughout Quaker history, this authority of personal experience was previously balanced by an equal reliance
on scriptural authority and the testing of the community in the
gathered meeting for worship. But in the latter half of the nine-

4 See Ben Pink Dandelion, *The Quakers: A very short introduction*
(Oxford: Oxford University Press, 2008), pp.65–70.

teenth century the traditional authority of scripture began to be undermined, firstly by biblical scholarship, textual criticism and archaeological discoveries, and subsequently by emerging scientific disciplines, especially evolutionary biology and geology[5].

The second tenet of liberal Quakerism is that faith must be relevant to the age. This search for relevance appears to reflect the tremendous expansion of scientific and industrial enterprise in the Victorian age, its hunger for discovery and global exploration based on Enlightenment principles of rationality and empirical enquiry. In this period, religious faith in the West starts to become subject to the same kind of experimental scrutiny as all other human endeavours.

The third tenet of liberal Quakerism opens the floodgates to an even greater change in direction for the Yearly Meeting during the twentieth century. Quaker faith, it is now argued, should be open to new light, and this links with a fourth tenet, which is that revelation is not only continuous – a traditional Quaker view – but also progressive. Mirroring the evolutionary, imperial, spirit of the age, the view now becomes established that current knowledge must be greater than (and therefore superior to) what was known previously.

These assumptions about Quaker faith that emerged in the late nineteenth century – that experience is primary, that the Quaker tradition will continue to evolve as each generation makes it relevant to their age, that Quakers should be open to new ideas, and that revelation has what Ben Pink Dandelion calls "a chronological authority" – became the guiding principles of twentieth century British Quakerism.

The influence of social and cultural change

In addition to the emergence of liberal Quakerism, other complex social and historical forces were at work that would profoundly affect the subsequent nature and evolution of the Quaker community in Britain. In the eighteenth and nineteenth centuries Quaker faith was maintained and transmitted mainly through close family relationships that were also networks of

5 For a more detailed account of this move away from biblical authority see my essay: Alex Wildwood, "Tradition & Transition: Opening to the sacred yesterday and today", *Woodbrooke Journal*, Winter 2001, No 9.

employment and of social and commercial bonds beyond the immediate family. During these centuries Friends could live their whole lives within the orbit of Quaker faith and values. But by the early twentieth century a growing proportion of those in membership of the Society were no longer "birthright" Friends, born into Quaker families. People began to be drawn from beyond this close-knit Quaker community for a number of reasons, including Friends' rejection of a doctrinal form of faith. Particularly following the horrors of World War I, people joined Friends through the growing reputation of Quakers as one of the peace churches – a religious body witnessing to disarmament and seeking to alleviate the suffering caused by war. Yet in spite of this changing membership, British Friends, however liberal their theology, continued to consider themselves an essentially Christian body for several further decades.

In the mid-twentieth century, however, the internal movement towards growing theological liberalism, combined with a marked shift in the wider culture, brought about a fundamentally new situation. In the 1960s there was a realignment in religious life in this country of such significance that social historian Callum Brown speaks of "the death of Christian Britain" occurring at this time.

In his study of religious life in Britain from 1800 to 2000[6], Brown challenges the conventional wisdom that industrialisation gave rise to a gradual process of increasing secularisation – and with it a similarly gradual decline in church attendance – from the mid-nineteenth into the twentieth century. Brown argues that parish records of this period reveal instead a sudden, dramatic collapse in church attendance and Christian affiliation occurring in the 1960s. During this decade younger women in particular, as part of their questioning of gender roles and identity, "cancelled their mass subscription" to the church. With so many women withdrawing from the social life of the church, this inevitably led to its declining influence in the community. Women had always played such a pivotal role in linking family life to the life of the parish that the breaking of that linkage led progressively to a "catastrophic collapse" of the influence of

---

6 Callum Brown, *The Death of Christian Britain: Understanding secularisation 1800–2000* (London: Routledge, 2001).

the established church in the life of the nation. Since the 1960s, Brown argues, we have seen, "not merely the continuing decline of organised Christianity, but the death of the culture that formerly conferred Christian identity upon the British people as a whole."

Brown describes how, from this point on in the twentieth century, "a suspicion of creeds arose that quickly took the form of a rejection of Christian tradition ..." While Christianity still claims a privileged role in the educational and ceremonial life of Britain – we remain a nominally Christian nation – for the majority of the population church religion has now become an irrelevance. Paradoxically, and coinciding with growth in spiritual diversity outside the church, the decline of the mainstream churches over the past five decades has played a part in the rise of the black-led churches, the house church movement and other expressions of evangelical Protestantism, while Catholic congregations have been strengthened by the influx of immigrants from Eastern Europe during this period.

The 1960s marked the end of what has been called the age of deference; it was then that the mass media started an escalating trend of portraying church religion as an object of scorn and derision. But other social factors contributed to the declining authority, influence and status of the established church from the 1960s. Most significant of these were the growing affluence of a post-war generation, the expansion of higher education giving rise to a culture of questioning and choice and, with growing numbers of immigrants from the former Empire, the emergence of Britain as a multicultural, multifaith society. Within roughly one generation – a remarkably short space of time – the centrality of Christian religion in the life of the nation had been called into question. Since the 1960s, the majority of people in Britain (and in advanced industrialised societies generally) have experienced a new-found freedom of choice in matters of religion – free to disassociate themselves from anything to do with the church, and free to choose their own religious or secular philosophy, their own way of imbuing life with meaning and purpose. The effects of these new social dynamics, portrayed in Callum Brown's stark assessment of the death of Christian Britain, are the essential context of the third and principal diagram of the model.

In Diagram 3 overleaf, the circle on the left-hand side representing the Christian tradition includes a few examples of the many ways Christianity in Britain has developed over the last half century – with the rise of evangelical and other Christian renewal movements in particular. On the right-hand side of the diagram is a suggestion of the religious, spiritual and secular diversity that has arisen or become more visible with the virtual collapse of the authority and influence of the established church since the 1960s. These other-than-Christian worldviews have had a growing influence on British society as a whole in the last five decades; the purpose of this diagram and the next is to illustrate the particular effect of this influence on the development of British Quakerism.

From the 1960s on, Friends and those drawn to Quakerism are increasingly aware of, and influenced by, a wide spectrum of spiritual paths, secular philosophies and worldviews – including other great faith traditions, but also humanism, non-theism and atheism. For some Friends, accommodating these other paths challenges previously held assumptions about Quakerism as essentially Christian. But this increased awareness among Friends also begins to affect Quakerism more generally. With their belief in continuing (progressive) revelation, their lack of a common creed as a basis for membership and their understated, simple forms of religious worship, Quakers in the latter half of the twentieth century and since have been particularly open to the new light coming from these many and varied influences.

Defining a new reality

It was the Quaker religious journalist and broadcaster Gerald Priestland who, in the 1970s, observed that people in the West were becoming "less and less religious and more and more spiritual" (an observation we explore in greater depth in later chapters). He was drawing attention to what we can now identify as a pronounced shift in religious culture in the West since the 1960s.

The past five decades or so have seen the emergence of a varied tapestry of beliefs and understandings that now inform the faith of British Friends. Increasingly in that time, Quaker meetings in Britain have become havens for a great variety of spiritual seekers – from those who have rejected church religion to those who are drawn to Friends' involvement in campaigns for justice, peace and the environment. As a religious society, Friends have tended to attract those who acknowledge some sense of the transcendent, but the simplicity and inclusivity of liberal Quakerism has also appealed to those who are aware of a need for "something spiritual" in their lives but who want nothing to do with the trappings of formal religion.

The right-hand side of diagram 3 includes an indication of the influences now available to such seekers. These examples of "postmodern" diversity give us a flavour of the many spiritual, religious and secular movements that have arisen out of the cultural changes of the last half-century, some of which are recent expressions of older traditions shaped by the contemporary context of questioning and experimentation. The diagram is not intended to imply that these diverse influences form a distinct entity, other than in seeing them collectively as an expression of postmodernity – with its rejection of a single orthodoxy or image of reality and its embracing of multiple and sometimes contradictory viewpoints. But complex though this concept is to define, in words or in a diagram, postmodern diversity of influence on spiritual and religious identity is something that people readily recognise and identify with from personal experience.

When describing this amalgam of worldviews and philosophies to participants on the project, I would speak of my own experience of varied spiritual influences – of the importance to me of feminist spirituality, Jungian depth psychology, aboriginal and pagan Earth-centred traditions, of elements of engaged Buddhism, transpersonal psychology and Twelve Step recovery fellowships. All of which have influenced my faith as much as (probably more than) traditional Christianity. I recognised parallels with my experience in a significant milestone in the life of the Yearly Meeting – the 1988 Swarthmore lecture, *A Minority of One*, in which Harvey Gillman, a Jewish Friend, described his own "journey amongst Friends" as a complex mosaic of influences and identities. His story spoke powerfully of how individuals from other faith traditions were being drawn to Friends and finding a spiritual home there. What Harvey Gillman and numerous others were finding in Friends was a welcome degree of awareness and openness borne of the way Quakerism in Britain – because of the liberalism of its theology – had come to reflect the cultural-religious changes happening in the wider culture.

46

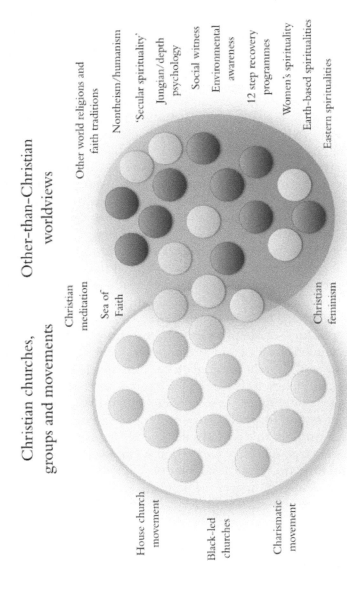

Christian churches, groups and movements

Other-than-Christian worldviews

House church movement

Black-led churches

Charismatic movement

Christian meditation

Sea of Faith

Christian feminism

Other world religions and faith traditions

Nontheism/humanism

'Secular spirituality'

Jungian/depth psychology

Social witness

Environmental awareness

12 step recovery programmes

Women's spirituality

Earth-based spiritualities

Eastern spiritualities

Diagram 3: Growth and increase in awareness of religious and spiritual diversity in Britain since the 1960s
N.B. Examples listed are illustrative only and not intended to be comprehensive

Evidence of these changes can be readily found in any high street. Whereas previously the spiritual seeker wanting books on the subject would have been lucky to find a couple of different versions of the Bible or a few Christian classics, since the 1980s the sections of any sizeable bookshop have included one that is often broadly labelled "Mind/Body/Spirit". On these shelves all faiths and wisdom traditions are represented. Here New Age and esoteric titles rub shoulders with the scriptures of all the major faiths. We have become so accustomed to this fact that it is easy to overlook its significance. As Robert Forman, Professor of Comparative Religions at Hunter College, New York, describes, "There has never before been an era in which every single major religious tradition is readily available to any educated person."[7]

This pluralism of our religious lives in the West, and the context of diversity in which every faith community in Britain now operates, present challenges and opportunities Quakers have not had to grapple with before. From one viewpoint this contemporary diversity simply reflects the triumph of market economics in our globalised world, in which even religious faith can now be seen as just another commodity, with each religious or faith group merely another "brand" competing for people's loyalty and attention. As "spiritual shoppers"[8] we are free to choose a given "product" or simply move on. But this pluralism, which is both a consequence of and a response to the dramatic decline in mainstream church congregations, also speaks of people's growing confidence to explore and express their sense of the numinous in new, more personally meaningful ways. So alongside the growth of formerly fringe or minority groups within the Christian tradition, this period since the 1960s also sees a growing number of people choosing to define themselves – as Gerald Priestland foresaw – as spiritual but not religious. This shift away from organised religion over the past five decades has been characterised by sociologist David Tacey as "the spirituality revolution"[9]. Various commentators use the term "the new spirituality"

7 Robert Forman, *Grassroots Spirituality: What it is, why it's here, where it's going* (Exeter: Imprint Academic, 2004).

8 The title of a television series broadcast in the UK in 2005.

9 David Tacey, *The Spirituality Revolution: The emergence of contemporary spirituality* (Hove: Brunner-Routledge, 2004).

to refer to how increasing numbers of people in the West are exploring their own blend of different spiritual influences.

"The Whole Banana"

Having described in the previous chapter the eclectic mix of aspects of postmodern diversity that I identify as significant in my own spiritual journey, it is important to point out that in any group Tim and I worked with, many Friends could immediately name the other-than-Christian influences in their own spiritual formation. This is where opportunity for real dialogue about diversity among Friends lies, because Quakers now occupy a very particular – almost certainly unique – place in the broader picture of religious and spiritual diversity in contemporary society. While many British Friends continue to find meaning and relevance in the Christian roots of Quakerism, others see no contradiction today in describing themselves as Jewish-Quakers, Buddhist-Quakers or Pagan-Quakers. For some, Quakerism provides the opportunity for seeking a new religious language for the divine, while for a significant minority of British Friends the overtly religious dimension of Quakerism is now only of historical interest and has nothing to do with their own search for truth, including Friends whose spiritual journey has led them away from belief in God altogether. The "Sea of Faith" movement is a notable example of a religious network that straddles the Christian boundary line in its attitude towards belief in God. In its conferences and publications it seeks to counter "the great danger in objectifying our God-concept into a supernatural Being". This movement, which describes its mission as "exploring and promoting religious faith as a human creation", includes in its membership a significant number of British Friends.

Within the Yearly Meeting, other Friends give expression to what has been called secular spirituality in their various kinds of activism – with civil liberties, feminist or environmental campaigning or work with refugees and asylum-seekers being both their point of contact with Quakers and the way in which their spiritual experience is discovered and expressed. Today the membership of Britain Yearly Meeting also includes those for whom the basis of their spirituality might be holistic healing practices, various schools of psychotherapy, or more broadly what psychologist David Elkins[10] calls "alternative paths to the sacred" – soul-work, the arts, spending time in nature, mythology and story-telling.

When I first began to share the model (with students on the Equipping for Ministry programme at Woodbrooke) I spontaneously drew an elongated shape overlaid on the third diagram to represent British Quakerism today, stretching between the Christian tradition on one side and the other-than-Christian worldviews on the other. The freehand outline I drew immediately reminded people of a banana and, for better or for worse, that title for the model, "The Quaker Banana", has since stuck. For me, what is useful as well as memorable about the image in Diagram 4 is that it refers to something distinct, a tangible entity defined by a boundary (the skin of the banana) and therefore having its own integrity. The shape of the banana image also suggests that diversity is a feature of Quakerism at every point along the spectrum, not just at the other-than-Christian end, or at the crossover point in the middle. It is important to note the real diversity amongst those who would readily describe themselves as Christian Quakers. As a metaphor for contemporary liberal Quakerism, the emphasis is on the whole banana; implicit in this image is a Quakerism that is rooted in Christianity and open to new light from beyond that tradition. In its current pluralist phase it is a faith that gains strength and maintains its integrity from being both/and, not either/or.

And the model – for all its light-hearted imagery – does pose some serious questions for British Friends: Can they accept and celebrate the complexity of their spiritual diversity without making light of the challenges and difficulties it presents? What holds the Quaker community together given the diverse beliefs of individual Friends? In terms of the model, what defines the skin of the banana? And what might be required of Friends – wherever they locate themselves within the Quaker banana – if they are to achieve true *unity in diversity*?

10 David Elkins, *Beyond Religion: 8 alternative paths to the sacred* (Wheaton, IL: Quest Books, 1998).

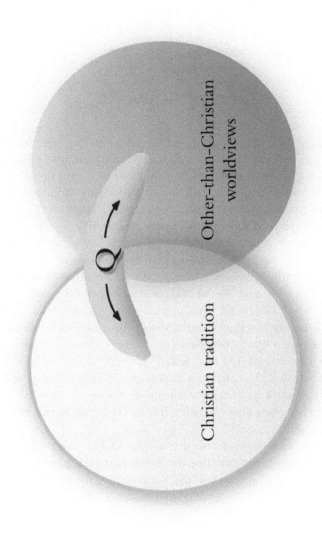

Diagram 4: The Quaker community rooted in the
Christian tradition and open to a wide range of influences

Chapter 4
Creating faith

Timothy Ashworth

All through the history sketched by Alex in the last chapter, Quakers can lay claim to persevering with a radical reforming Christian social agenda. In the eighteenth and nineteenth centuries they took practical action to abolish slavery, to improve the conditions for prisoners and those suffering from mental illness, to create improved living and working conditions for factory workers, and to relieve the catastrophic effects of starvation in Ireland during the potato famine. In the last century they were involved in getting Jewish children away from Germany and Austria before the Second World War, and later played a major part in the founding of several humanitarian organisations including Oxfam, Amnesty International and the Alternatives to Violence Project. Recently Quakers have been active in developing ways of enabling those convicted of a sexual offence to return to life in the community with a support and accountability group. Effective practical work in areas often outside the reach of more conventional churches and charities has been a distinctive feature of Quaker life.

It is not hard to read into this action a Christian motivation. Is this not putting into practice the Sermon on the Mount, or the words of Jesus that "just as you did these things to one of the least of my brothers and sisters, you did it to me"? The recognition of the profound compatibility of this work with the Christian Gospel has meant that, although Quakers do not as a matter of principle profess a credal understanding of Jesus, they are welcome in local and national ecumenical bodies.

Many Friends do indeed turn to the example and teaching of Jesus for inspiration. Others look to the Quaker testimonies to equality, simplicity, truth and peace as a way of becoming clear about the kinds of activity Friends should be initiating and sustaining in any contemporary situation. Yet both these approaches, however worthy and useful, do not get to the heart of what motivates Quaker action. In the Quaker tradition, the testimonies and the actions and teaching of Jesus, while they certainly do provide inspiration for action, are all better understood as ways of confirming the rightness of a particular activity rather than as its motivating source.

I found it very helpful to discover how Quaker action is integrally bound up with Quaker worship. From my perspective, meeting for worship is a space created for hearing the voice of the prophet, that is, one who speaks in the power of the Spirit. This is the space from which new initiatives spring, and where those initiatives are tested by the community. In this way, Friends sometimes find themselves uniting around a voice from the margins, a voice that is eventually recognised as expressing something that needs to be firmly spoken and acted upon by the whole Quaker community for the good of the wider world.

Over the whole of Christian history – not just Quaker history – just such a marginal voice has been heard and has led individuals to act. It has prompted renewal; it has led to new expressions of Christian community, new social actions. But repeatedly throughout Christian history that prophetic voice has been in a stormy and sometimes violent relationship with the institutional elements of the church. By contrast, a distinctive feature of Friends is that a structure was created that enabled the living prophetic voice to remain at the centre of the community, but framed in practices that provide gentle but firm disciplines of discernment. Because of this, the authoritative heart of the community did not come to be represented by any special book or individual but, in both principle and practice, is found in and through every member of the community.

Early Friends called these structures "Gospel Order", convinced they were replicating similar structures in the early church. Through the work of modern biblical scholarship we are now better placed than ever before to see how accurate a description that was. Scholarship has proceeded to show more clearly how the credal understanding of Jesus comes about after the time of the New Testament. But in the earliest days, before the texts were written and gathered, direct dramatic experiences of the Spirit lay behind the claims those first Christian communities made for Jesus.

Faith and the living word

The history of the people of Israel was blessed with great individuals who, sometimes against their own will, felt themselves taken hold of by God's Spirit. The definition of a prophet is one who speaks by divine inspiration. The Hebrew scriptures have plenty of references to how literally that was understood. The refrain "thus says the Lord" is so familiar in conventional Christianity that we can miss its bold implication: the prophet becomes the mouth of the Lord. The understanding is that God's word sounds through the individual who speaks. The fact that the words prophets are given to speak do not necessarily enhance their standing is itself an indication of authenticity. Sometimes prophets suffer, as the words they bring are not comfortable ones and often involve challenging injustice and the misuse of power by king or priest. It is in the light of this history that Jesus himself is seen in his own time as a prophet.

The acknowledgement of that fact is itself a scholarly breakthrough. For so many generations it has been impossible to see Jesus without the overlay of the later claims of the church, claims that are already being made by the time the Gospels are written. But many scholars can now unite around the picture of Jesus as a Jewish prophet.

Scholarship is gradually showing more clearly how prophecy had a central place in the early Christian community, with one crucial distinction from the Jewish story up to that point. Previously, the sense of prophetic inspiration had come upon individuals who were identified as having a special calling. The claim of the early church, the claim Peter is presented as making at the time of Pentecost – a matter of weeks after the death of Jesus – is that God's Spirit is being poured out not on special individuals but on the whole community. This was seen as the fulfilment of the prophecy that when God's reign came, all would feel the power of God's Spirit, all would prophesy. This is why John's Gospel speaks frequently of the "voice" that is recognised by the true followers of Jesus. This is the voice of prophecy now at work in the community.

The clearest support for this Quaker understanding of the early Christian community comes in Paul who describes an early gathering of the community. He has already made it clear he believes God is speaking in the community. What he is then concerned with is how that living voice is best heard and understood.

> Let two or three prophets speak, and let the others weigh what is said. If a revelation is made to someone else sitting nearby, let the first person be silent. For you can all prophesy one by one, so that all may learn and all be encouraged. (1 Cor 14: 29–31)

It is in this context of access to the living word, an access that most of Paul's fellow Jews could not accept was happening, that Paul speaks of being guided by a "living faith" in contrast to the "written law".

This picture of a new intimacy with God's Spirit for all people becomes even more vivid when we see that in several places where Paul's words have traditionally been translated "faith in Jesus", they can equally well, and more naturally, be translated, "faith of Jesus" (Rom 3:22, 26; Gal 2:16, 20; Phil 3:9). Where Paul has been held to be saying that "God makes right the one who has faith in Jesus", there is now strong scholarly support for a different translation: "God liberates the one who has the faith of Jesus" (Rom 3:26).

Friends I have worked with at Woodbrooke have been quick to recognise the implications of interpreting Paul in this way. It replaces a cornerstone for exclusive truth claims for the Christian tradition with a concept that is open and dramatically inclusive. "Only faith in Jesus will save you" is readily associated with beliefs about Jesus, a credal understanding in which the individual affirms key facts about Jesus. The view that what liberates us is faith *as seen* in Jesus suggests that faith operates at a different level from ideas that can be believed in. Instead of seeing Jesus as occupying a distant high place, prayed to and worshipped (which is the understanding of Jesus that probably shaped the way Paul's simple genitive phrase was translated), faith is the disposition of heart and mind that Jesus lived with, and that now others can also participate in.

What is more, it suggests that a person who is not Christian can have the same kind of trusting faith that Jesus had. Indeed, with this interpretation, the faith of Jesus could be demonstrated in the words and actions of someone who has never heard of Jesus, someone from another religious tradition or none.

Christian roots: not avoiding the challenge

There is no question that this understanding of faith has opened doors for many people, enabling them to approach or re-engage with Jesus and the Christian tradition. However, I am always aware as people warmly embrace this interpretation that, although it can have the effect of making Jesus more accessible, uncomfortable challenges are still lurking inside it for those who open themselves to its implications. For if we take seriously the picture of Jesus as a Spirit-led prophet, this invites us to look afresh at the significance of actions he took. Specifically, we have to give our attention to the way that he goes up to Jerusalem, towards a seemingly inevitable confrontation.

For me (and I am sure for many others involved with Friends) the opportunities for reflection provided by the church's year still carry significance and value. I write this on Maundy Thursday. This evening the three days at the heart of the church's life begin. From the traditional Christian point of view, as Sunday is to the rest of the week, these three days are for the whole year.

While I have not been a member for many years, I still have a foot in the Catholic Church. This evening I will go to the Mass of the Lord's Supper. With the Catholic community in Selly Oak, Birmingham, I will be present as we relive Jesus washing the feet of his disciples, celebrating the Passover meal with them and then going to the garden of Gethsemane. The mass will have no formal ending. Having walked around the church we will squeeze into a side chapel to be left there watching and praying with Jesus. Without formality, the rest of the church will be stripped of all decoration. People get up to go when they are ready. Some will stay until late into the night. The instructions for this service say: "all leave in silence".

In order to really appreciate the faith of Jesus, it is necessary to understand what was going on for Jesus on this night. How can we know? How can we get inside the mind of Jesus? Of course, we cannot. But for an event so long ago, of such little significance at the time, we have accounts that do not read like made up stories, accounts where the writers are concerned to pass on what they know even when they do not understand the significance of it. It is true that where they do have a sense of the meaning of something they may well elaborate so that we get the same message too, but for me, the core of the story rings true. And that may well be said by many readers who do not accept the historicity of the story in the way that I do. It is a story that is revealing of truth even when the facts are in dispute.

So what was going on? At the critical point I want to pay attention to here, Jesus left his disciples and went away on his own to pray. Three principles about the nature of faith are vital to our understanding of the faith of Jesus. Firstly, faith is rooted in freedom; it cannot be forced. Jesus can choose what happens. It is his deliberate actions that have brought him to this point. He can leave Gethsemane; he can leave Jerusalem. Secondly, and paradoxically, faith is not only about freedom but also about service. As a faithful Jew, Jesus is seeking to do the will of God. As a prophet who has had that calling validated by healings and revelations among those he has encountered, what he is listening for is what God requires of him. Thirdly, faith is not limited by the traditional forms of religion. What has brought Jesus to this point are the things he has said and done in the Temple in Jerusalem. The Temple occupied the central place in the religious life of the Jews, God's covenant people. Corruption there might have been, but people continued to flock to Jerusalem to pray and seek forgiveness and give thanks for God's blessings. Jesus has performed prophetic actions that, from the perspective of the Temple priests, interfere with the functioning of God's work. One simple reason for stopping him was in order to carry out their responsibility of ensuring that the Temple could continue the God-given tasks for which thousands of Jews came to Jerusalem.

After leaving his disciples in the garden at Gethsemane, Jesus the prophet is faced with being true to the word of God spoken in his heart as he "wrestles" in prayer. He is seeking to discern if he is truly called to do what he knows will be seen by some of his fellow Jews as a challenge to the word of God revealed over generations in the scriptures and rituals of his people. To be true to the God he has been following, through whom great things have happened around him, Jesus has to follow through the consequences of his prophetic acts in the Temple, acts that have shown him in some kind of opposition to what is happening there.

The Quaker tradition is better placed than any other to recognise what I think is the precise issue. Jesus has stayed true to his prophetic ministry, to the leadings of God, and it has taken him right into the Temple, the heart of Jewish life. Instead of being welcomed and finding recognition among the Temple authorities, he has provoked hostility. The very people whose task it is to oversee the work of God in the Temple cannot see in Jesus the Spirit that underlies all that they do. They do not start by wanting to oppose Jesus. This is the drama of Holy Week; he is probably from their point of view a relatively insignificant figure when he arrives, but in a sequence of prophetic actions he makes himself unavoidable. He faces the Temple priests with a decision that cannot be shirked if they are going to be true to their God-given task of sustaining the rites of the Temple. If they do not act, the Romans will. And the Romans have no interest in intervening in a manner that will avoid disrupting the workings of the Temple at Passover time.

Jesus is put to death in the most wretched way. In the last hours before he dies there is no sign for him or for others to show that he has God's blessing. There is no sign in his death that the Spirit is with him. To those who see him he looks and, as Matthew and Mark describe it, himself feels "God-forsaken". His death appears to give a definitive verdict on his controversial actions in Jerusalem: he was not acting in a way that was true to God. He has challenged the activity of God's Temple and his death seems to confirm that his authority was not from God, that he was not "Spirit-led".

Faith and creation

Alex and I have sometimes shown the film *Jesus of Montreal* as a lighter element of courses we have run at Woodbrooke. It has a mixture of drama and humour that encourages a different kind of reflection on the figure of Jesus and on wider religious themes. Towards the end of the film, an official has the job of bringing to an abrupt end an acted performance of the Passion just as Jesus has been put on the cross. The audience do not want to leave and someone shouts, "We want to see the end!" at which the official says, "We all know the end. He dies. He resurrects. Where's the mystery there?" The opportunity and challenge of working with the Bible among Friends is that, as with any element of the Christian tradition, there is no requirement to "believe in" the resurrection. It has to make some kind of sense in terms of practice or experience, and this can make possible a fresh approach.

So it was that during our work together Alex would frequently challenge me not to avoid the crunch issue: what about the resurrection? I know that his desire in asking this was to try and get to the heart of the Christian faith, to find out from me why I find it difficult to simply list Jesus as one of the great spiritual teachers. But he was also genuinely interested to know how the resurrection connects with the witness and worship of Friends.

A preliminary point that has to be to taken seriously is the extremity of Jesus' failure. It is not surprising that at first Jesus' disciples flee or hide. All their hopes and expectations have been proved mistaken. Recognising this has to precede any attempt to understand what it is that transforms their fear into an unshakeable boldness.

I could legitimately evade Alex's challenge, and even justify not introducing this topic here at all, by mentioning that the most prominent recent book on the resurrection[1] is 817 pages long! Nevertheless, I think there are some things that can be said reasonably briefly, and they may help readers reflect on this central element of the Christian story and tradition and how it may still be significant for Friends.

A concept I have found valuable in understanding the impact Jesus had both in his own life and subsequently is expansion. One well-known aspect of Jesus' life is that he deliberately went out of his way to meet and spend time with those who were the outcasts of his society. The authenticity of the words "he eats with tax collectors and sinners" (Mt 9:11; 11:19; Mk 2:15; Lk 5:30; 7:34; 15:1) is virtually unchallenged among scholars. His teaching in relation to these actions confirms their importance for understanding his purpose. He is acting upon his own sense that God's blessing is not limited by, but expands beyond, the boundaries of religious law. This is the faith of Jesus in action,

1 N. T. Wright, *The Resurrection of the Son of God* (London: SPCK, 2003).

doing what God requires even when this looks like disobedience to the "God-given" Law of Moses.

After his death, his followers demonstrate a similarly expanded sense of God's blessing. They act upon what they believe are the signs and promptings of the Spirit to embrace non-Jews, people who were by definition beyond the boundaries of God's blessing.

In Mark's Gospel, followed by Matthew and Luke, at the moment of Jesus' death, the veil of the Temple is "torn in two, from top to bottom" (15:38). This is the curtain separating off the "holy of holies", the dwelling place of God on Earth, and it is difficult to imagine a more powerful sign within the Jewish tradition for God's holy power, God's blessing, expanding out beyond the religious boundaries centred upon Temple and Law.

Within only a few years after the death of Jesus, Paul is saying to the predominantly non-Jewish community in Corinth: "Do you not know that you are God's temple and that God's Spirit dwells in you?" (1 Cor 3:16). Familiarity with the idea contained in this text can prevent us feeling its significance. What is being affirmed here is something that is expressed in a whole variety of ways in the Christian scriptures: just as God's Spirit could be confidently found in the Temple with access to it through the sacrifices done by the priests, God's Spirit can now be seen dwelling in those who live by faith, whether Jew or Gentile. Acts of the Apostles begins with the account of the Spirit being poured out on Peter and his friends in Jerusalem who now are described as "filled with the Spirit". The letters of John have some of the most well known expressions of the indwelling of the Spirit: "By this we know that we abide in him and he in us, because he has given us of his Spirit. ... God is love, and those who abide in love abide in God, and God abides in them." (1 John 4:13, 16)

How does this help in approaching the resurrection? There are two things that the resurrection accounts describe as being "seen": the empty tomb and Jesus alive. While accounts of the empty tomb are elaborated with visions of angels, the very first witness is to the simple fact that the body of Jesus had gone from the tomb. The appearances of Jesus are more strange. All the accounts are concerned to show that Jesus is not just a spiritual presence. There is some kind of physical reality to what people see but it is not simply a dead body brought back to life. Jesus is sometimes suddenly in the midst of them. In one brief picture in Matthew's Gospel, some in the group are on their knees while others have doubts about what is happening. His presence has been described as "more-than-physical", that is, not simply a "spiritual" presence but not simply "physical" either.

Two effects of the resurrection appearances tend to be the ones most noted and discussed. In the first place the resurrection affirms the power of God over death. It is not that the story of the resurrection introduces a belief in life after death; such a belief was almost universal at the time. Rather, and this is a topic that can be dwelt on at length, it is that death, as a fact of human life, need no longer be a source of fear, because the blessing of God transcends death. In the second place, it affirms that Jesus was indeed God's prophet, one who is speaking and acting in God's power. In the eyes of those who witnessed his death, the value of Jesus' life was reduced to nothing on the cross, but the resurrection Spirit now vindicates all his teaching and action. It is all seen as God's work, and from that time to this stories about him have been retold and learnt from. Of course, in the retelling of those stories there quickly comes to be more said about Jesus than simply relaying the facts of his life. The resurrection accounts describe Jesus as being worshipped. Very soon after the events, far more exalted titles than "prophet" are given to him. Ways of speaking of him emerge that express his closeness to God: at God's right hand; God's son; the wisdom of God; God's wisdom or word made flesh.

These titles reflect the devotion that came to be felt towards Jesus. It is these titles that come to the fore as the church grows, with its preaching, prayer and worship. But these developments tend to obscure an understanding of what Jesus brought about that early Friends rediscovered, and which the style of Quaker worship still points to. The miracle of the resurrection remains only part fulfilled if it is limited to seeing Jesus as the only son of God in human flesh, as the one who is exalted into the heavens and worshipped, while his followers struggle far beneath him. For the very first Christians, what happened to Jesus was only the beginning of what God was doing. In order to explain a bit more of what the resurrection might mean to Friends, it is worth drawing out a further dimension of that evocative image of the curtain of the holy of holies torn in two, something that might appear too primitive for the modern reader of the Bible accounts to take seriously.

The English word "revelation" contains within it the same sense as the Greek word that it translates. To *reveal* is to *remove a veil or curtain* so that something can be seen that was previously hidden. In a revelation, what is seen changes the person who sees it. Quite clearly, the resurrection accounts are describing moments of revelation. The holy of holies represents a belief in God's holy power having a "place" in the world. While the image of the torn curtain does dramatically represent expansion, it does not challenge that fundamental Jewish understanding of God: God choosing the people of Israel, travelling with them through the desert and dwelling among them in a special way in the Temple. The expansion it is representing is not out from the holy of holies into an undefined universal "spiritual" reality. What the witnesses of the resurrection come to proclaim is the invisible Spirit of God expanding into humankind in all its visible, fleshly physicality.

This is why the Christian tradition has continued to affirm that the resurrection of Jesus was not simply a spiritual revelation, and why so much is made of the physical nature of the events: the empty tomb and the physical but more-than-physical appearances of Jesus. In seeing the Spirit definitively revealed in Jesus resurrected, those who witnessed this were perceiving a new way of being human, a new way that was not simply observation but actual participation in this "new creation".

The presence of God's Spirit in the physical reality of the body is made clear in several texts from Paul: "Do you not know that your body is a temple of the Holy Spirit within you, which you have from God ...?" (1 Cor 6:19); "If the Spirit of him who raised Jesus from the dead dwells in you he who raised Christ from the dead will give life to your mortal bodies also through his Spirit that dwells in you" (Rom 8:11).

As noted earlier, such texts are so familiar to the many who have been brought up in the Christian tradition that the radical nature of the claims that are implicit within them can be missed. The idea that the body of the one who lives by faith is the place where the Spirit of God dwells and works is not simply presented as a pious aspiration; it is stated to be the new situation. The early Christian claims arise from and rest on this experience. It is why the tradition speaks of God and humankind now reconciled, why Paul's letters are full of the language of transformation.

It is this spirit of transformation that the first Quakers also felt. Having gone through their own experience of the cross, in which all that separated them from God was revealed to them but also healed, they came to a new confidence that life in the Spirit was a reality. Their sense that "Christ has come to teach his people himself" was a vivid experience of Christ in the midst of the community, teaching and leading and inspiring them as individuals and as a group to be God's presence in the world. In the earliest days, and in much of subsequent Quaker history, the lack of external forms in Quaker worship has not been in any sense a downplaying of the significance of Jesus but rather a new experience of his presence in the midst of the members of the community. This was the experience that fundamentally shifted their perspective from worshipping that which is "outside" to living in the power of that which is "within" and "among" them.

From my Christian perspective, all the work of Friends to heal the world has been the Quaker witness to the resurrection. To live with "the faith of Jesus", open to the word of God in the present, is to live our physical lives in the power of the Spirit. As early Friends affirmed, it is this power of God working in and through people that Jesus reveals. They enjoined everyone they encountered not to simply read about it but to be open to this liberating way of faith for themselves. To live by faith is to live by the power of the Spirit and become the human hands and feet through which God's creative power can work to transform the world.

Chapter 5

Faith in transition

Alex Wildwood

When I was asked to give the Swarthmore Lecture in 1999, I found it hard to imagine how an account of my own spiritual journey could warrant such a privileged platform within the Yearly Meeting, but in travelling amongst Friends since I have come to appreciate why, I think, the lecture committee were led to give me such a task. One of the things people have responded to most enthusiastically in my lecture was when I described how we enjoy today a freedom to question and explore matters of faith and spirituality scarcely imaginable to previous generations. Christianity no longer exerts the monopoly on the religious imagination of the population that it once did, both for the historical reasons outlined in Chapter 3 and because, in more recent times, modern communications, global travel and migration, education and the media have all greatly increased people's awareness of the various faith traditions of the world – many of which are now part of our multicultural society. With Christianity no longer assumed to be the default religion of British culture, spiritual seekers of all kinds, including Friends, now feel free to discover in their own way what feels right for them.

For Friends in Britain there is a paradox in this new freedom: Quaker faith does not require adherence to Christian belief and it does support Friends in being *open to new light* – to discover from experience what is true for them, and yet it is a faith community that draws particular nourishment both from its Christian history and from the Christian faith of many of its members. The effect of this paradox is a tension, held collectively by Friends, between the historical fact of being rooted in Christianity and the contemporary reality of Quaker spiritual diversity.

It is in this sense that I would describe British Quakers as a community in transition, corporately reflecting a process of change happening in religious and spiritual life more widely. In the absence of appointed clergy to maintain an orthodoxy of belief or practice, the Quaker commitment to continuous revelation has made British Quakers particularly susceptible to the influence of changes in the wider religious culture of Britain over the past five decades. This process of change is felt especially in the matter of whether Friends now view themselves as an essentially Christian body. In their Epistle from Junior Yearly Meeting in 2008, Young Friends observed: "It would appear that Quakerism is changing, in that the links between Christianity and Quakerism are existent but not compulsory." If this trend of weakening links continues, at some point Friends will inevitably face the question of whether Quakerism could maintain its integrity *independently* of those roots. Young Friends seem to be more comfortable with such a possibility than the Yearly Meeting as a whole, but it is already clear that the Religious Society of Friends is now a body in which some Quakers identify as Christian and others do not. While this issue seems less prominent in the life of the Yearly Meeting than it did some years ago,[1] the tension about Friends' fundamental religious identity remains, and can be a source of difficulty or conflict within local and area meetings.

Spiritual but not religious

If there were no other factors involved, this situation would not represent diversity, just a difference between two kinds of Friends – Christian and non-Christian. However, there are a number of other dichotomies present in the make-up of British Friends today that add greatly to the complexity of the picture of Quaker spiritual diversity. Towards the end of this chapter I shall return to the dichotomy between those for whom God is

1 See for instance accounts of the debate between the Christocentric and universalist positions in Alistair Heron, Ralph Hetherington and Joseph Pickvance, *The State of the Yearly Meeting: Where do we seem to be*, (London: Quaker Home Service and Woodbrooke, 1994).

a reality underpinning their faith and those who have no belief in God. Here I want to look more closely at the distinction that is increasingly made between religion and spirituality – a distinction that is evident in the language Quakers choose to use. Though it is hard to generalise, it is noticeable that many British Friends are more comfortable to speak and write about *the Spirit* or *Spirit* rather than *God*; while some Friends would like to change the title *Religious Society of Friends* because of the connotations the word "religion" has acquired.

Historically, spirituality has referred to the deepest, most central and inward element of religion, and to its lived expression in everyday life. It also referred, specifically, to the practice of prayer and devotional exercises by clerics or other religious[2]. These days, spirituality is widely used in a popular, inclusive sense, to cover, as Australian sociologist David Tacey[3] puts it, "all pathways that lead to meaning and purpose". Christian theologian John Drane[4] notes that, especially since the attacks on the World Trade Center on September 11th, 2001, religion has increasingly come to be associated in the popular imagination with fanaticism, irrationality and violence; at a subjective level it is perceived to be an imposed worldview and set of practices. Far from serving our noblest aspirations, religion – in this new popular sense of the word – is now seen by many people in the West as an obstacle to growth or liberation, an archaic system of rules and regulations belonging to a bygone age. Spirituality, on the other hand, is seen as something life enhancing and empowering to the individual, a means of realising our full potential and an aid to living at peace with oneself, other people and the planet. What David Tacey, John Drane and other commentators refer to as "The new spirituality" is a movement that sees itself as promoting healing and wholeness, and one that seeks to do away with the traditional separations of body–mind and matter–spirit.

2 See Philip Sheldrake, *A Brief History of Spirituality* (Oxford: Blackwell, 2007).

3 David Tacey, *The Spirituality Revolution: The emergence of contemporary spirituality* (Hove: Brunner-Routledge, 2004).

4 John Drane, *Do Christians Know How to be Spiritual? The rise of new spirituality and the mission of the Church* (London: Darton, Longman & Todd, 2005).

David Tacey describes the "cultural-religious revolution" of the last few decades as a spontaneous movement in society that reflects "a new interest in the reality of spirit and its healing affect on life, health, community and well-being". Significantly, the new spirituality seeks to embrace scientific understandings, recognising that "recent discoveries in physics, biology, psychology, and ecology have begun to restore dignity to previously discredited spiritual visions of reality". In this contemporary, broader, sense of spirituality, Tacey observes, "people replace loyalty to their natal faith with a new kind of loyalty to their inner striving or personal spiritual quest".

Unsurprisingly, not all commentators see these developments in a positive light. In *Selling Spirituality: The silent takeover of religion*, authors Jeremy Carrette and Richard King[5] argue that spirituality has become merely another powerful commodity in the global market place. What they describe as "the privatisation of religion" reflects how the market mentality has now infiltrated all aspects of our lives in advanced industrialised societies. This critical view echoes the observation attributed to G.K. Chesterton that "When people stop believing in God, they don't believe in nothing – they believe in anything." New Age spirituality in particular – just one form of this contemporary exploration of spirituality but perhaps its most attention-grabbing expression – has been criticised for being shallow, self-indulgent and narcissistic.

What Quakers, with their experiential sense of faith, can bring to this debate between the enthusiasm of those attracted to anything new and vaguely spiritual, and the scepticism of those with a more detached or hostile view is their tradition of testimony, of spirituality as engagement with the world. Friends have never seen personal spiritual development as separate from their service to others.

In her book *The Tao of Contemplation*, Jasmin Lee Cori[6] speaks of the two journeys of the self in which we are all engaged; the first is the journey of self-development and self-awareness whilst

5 Jeremy Carrette & Richard King, *Selling Spirituality: The silent takeover of religion* (London: Routledge, 2005).

6 Jasmin Lee Cori, *The Tao of Contemplation: Re-sourcing the inner life* (York Beach, ME: Samuel Weiser, 2000).

the second is the journey of self-forgetting or self-transcendence. Traditionally, therapy and personal growth have focused on the former and spiritual disciplines on the latter. A feature common to many of the contemporary explorations of spirituality is fluidity between these two paths. For Friends, their testimonies – the way Quakers seek to live their lives – are held to be an expression of the spiritual life; in other words, they integrate the spiritual discipline of service with personal spiritual growth.

A different way of being religious

William Bloom[7] is a leading proponent of what he calls "holistic spirituality", which, he says, "welcomes and respects that there are many ways of exploring the meaning, purpose and mystery of life – all of them equally valid". Spiritual authority, he suggests, is not something outside us; we do not need to go to "external teachers, lessons, icons, faiths, systems" to explore or deepen our spiritual experience. "We need only to come home, to the very fabric of our bodies and selves ... There is no separation between the material and the spiritual; the only issue is where we put our attention."

Varied as contemporary expressions of spirituality may seem to be, what they have in common are certain processes, forms and ways of working – the practice of which has the effect of bringing people together in community. In the new spirituality communities grow from sharing a journey rather than agreed formulations of faith. Seekers in the new spirituality movement try to integrate traditional dichotomies between body–mind and matter–spirit through such diverse activities as sacred dance, self-healing groups, rituals to mark life-transitions, study and support groups focusing on particular life challenges or on eco-political activism. In such groups, participants are encouraged to share from personal experience in a feeling-centred, intimate way, as people discover and affirm together their own deepest values. This style of peer support group, the mode of intimate sharing from personal experience, the inclusion of the emotional and the bodily as aspects of the sacred, have their origins in the second wave of the women's movement in the

7 William Bloom, *Soulution: The holistic manifesto* (Carlsbad, CA, and London: Hay House Inc., 2004).

mid-twentieth century and in women's honouring of more intuitive and relational ways of understanding.

An example of the influence of these trends within Britain Yearly Meeting can be seen by comparing the Woodbrooke study materials *Gifts & Discoveries* produced in the 1980s, with those of the *Hearts & Minds Prepared* study pack of 2004. While *Gifts & Discoveries* was based mainly on reading instructive "expert" texts as the basis for discussion, *Hearts & Minds Prepared* placed much greater reliance on a group process based on sharing from personal experience. This marked difference in learning style between the two sets of resources reflects a change in outlook towards an increasing awareness among Friends of the central importance of their own experiences and the value of experimenting with processes by which these might be explored.

"Humble learners in the school of Christ"
At heart, the dialogue between Tim and myself has always been about where the contemporary spirituality movement can dialogue with radical interpretations of the Christian tradition on our common ground of liberal Quakerism. Through our ongoing conversations I have come to a deeper appreciation of how Friends' rootedness in Christianity is best understood as a community's attempt to be faithful to the Way of Jesus. Intellectually, I accept that a relationship to Jesus, of the kind Tim describes in the previous chapter, has been at the heart of Quaker worship and witness since the seventeenth century – and remains so to this day for the great majority of Friends worldwide. But so far, that relationship has not been part of my own faith experience. While the Quaker understanding of what Tim describes as the faith *of* Jesus clearly derives from the gospels, the experience of many Friends, myself included, witnesses to the fact that it can also be approached intuitively from entirely other directions.

The following extract from Edgar G. Dunstan's 1956 Swarthmore Lecture[8] comes from the period when the assumed Christian basis of Britain Yearly Meeting first begins to move towards the spiritual diversity we find today. It amplifies for me how the

8 Edgar G. Dunstan, *Quakers and the Religious Quest* (London: George Allen & Unwin, 1956). Quoted in *Quaker Faith & Practice* 11.18.

Way of Jesus (the school of Christ) is a present rather than historic reality accessible to Christian and non-Christian alike.

> Our membership ... is never based upon worthiness... We none of us are members because we have attained a certain standard of goodness, but rather because, in this matter, we still are all humble learners in the school of Christ. Our membership is of no importance whatever unless it signifies that we are committed to something of far greater and more lasting significance than can adequately be conveyed by the closest association with any movement or organisation.

We can read in this reference to "humble learners" an implication that the inspiration Friends draw from their Christian heritage is responsive and changing, not dogmatic and fixed; that Friends are always in a process of spiritual discernment rather than a steady state of religious certainty. More than sixty years after Dunstan's lecture, Friends are still engaged in that process of discovering what is most essential about their Christian roots, and this seems to be a particularly exciting time to be considering such questions. As well as the recent scholarly work on early Christianity Tim has referred to, which is opening up our understanding of the Jesus of history, there has also been a spate of more popular authors[9] exploring the life and teachings of Jesus from the perspective of a contemporary, evolutionary understanding of spirituality and human consciousness.[10] Such writers demonstrate how Jesus can be a prophetic voice for those who want nothing to do with church religion.

It is implicit in the "whole banana" model that new light from anywhere represented in the diagram can illuminate anywhere

9 See, for instance, *Jesus for the Non-Religious* by John Shelby Spong (New York: Harper, 2007); *The Third Jesus: How to find truth and love in today's world* by Deepak Chopra (London: Rider, 2008); *Jesus for the Rest of Us* by John Selby (Charlottesville, VA: Hampton Roads, 2006); and *Your Forgotten Self Mirrored in Jesus the Christ* by David Robert Ord (Vancouver: Namaste Publishing, 2007).

10 See any of the books by Adrian B. Smith, his latest being *God, Energy & the Field* (Winchester: O Books, 2008). Particularly exciting in this regard is the "evolutionary spirituality" of Christian mystic Jim Marion; see *The Death of the Mythic God: The rise of evolutionary spirituality* (Charlottesville, VA: Hampton Roads, 2004).

else. This suggests, for example, that postmodern spiritualities can and do draw on the wisdom of older faith traditions (not only Christianity), and that the church is in turn being affected by new theologies, the processes being explored in the new spirituality, and, importantly, by a greater awareness of other faiths engendered by the natural commerce of our increasingly multifaith society. This "mutual irradiation"[11] of spiritual and religious cultures is made particularly visible in Quakerism because a large part of the spectrum of diverse beliefs and understandings can be found within the one faith community. This is a significant reason why some people find Friends a place of refuge from other churches: Quakerism attracts people looking for a different approach to religion or spirituality, while offering connectedness with valued cultural or religious roots.

The question of "God"

The banana model grew out of a dialogue between Tim's Christian and my non-Christian Quaker perspectives, but in considering the Yearly Meeting as a whole we need to include a further dimension in our model of Quaker diversity. This is the dimension Quaker Life Central Committee identified in its report to Meeting for Sufferings[12] in July 2008: "Whereas a generation ago the largest theological divide among us was expressed as between the Christ-centred and the universalist, it now appears to be between those whose experience is of a transcendent God and nontheists, for whom "God" is a metaphor for entirely human experience." While many Friends would still assert that belief in God is implicit in the practices of Quakerism, a significant number attending Meeting now identify themselves as non-theist, and less commonly, atheist or humanist, including Friends who have been welcomed into membership in the full knowledge of this as their faith position. Just as Christianity was the unquestioned basis of Quaker faith for all generations of Friends prior to the mid-twentieth century, so too was belief in God. Now we are seeing that alongside changes in the ways Friends draw on their Christian inheritance, the range and variety of understandings of God has expanded to include a view of

11 Douglas V. Steere, *Mutual Irraditation: A Quaker view of ecumenism* (Wallingford, PA: Pendle Hill Publications, 1971).
12 The representative body of Britain Yearly Meeting.

God as myth or metaphor.[13]

Undoubtedly some Friends find this development disheartening, disturbing or simply incomprehensible, but I want to suggest that there may be creative potential in it too. It offers Friends the opportunity to engage and explore with one another what God means to them, what images of the divine are meaningful for them, and how belief in God, or a concept of the sacred, influences their lives. Some of this exploring will inevitably be informed by ideas and concepts found in postmodern spiritualities or other faith traditions. Discovering new ways of imaging God, to better describe our experience of what a Friend spoke to me of as "a presence beyond ourselves", may well strengthen the core of Quakerism through the necessity of keeping this exploration in the foreground of Quaker faith and witness. Newcomers to Quaker meeting quite frequently comment on how hard it is to discover what Friends in fact believe, how "No-one tells you what to believe, you have to work it out for yourself." But this is also one of Quakerism's great attractions: it has the potential to speak directly to the cultural context of spiritual seekers today. This was certainly the founding impetus of Quaker Quest, the longest-running Quaker outreach programme of modern times, which has held weekly meetings in London since 2002 and has since spread to Australia, South Africa, the United States and Canada.

One way of imagining the diversity of understandings about God among Quakers today would be another version, or layer, of the banana model. If Friends located themselves within the Quaker banana – in relation to Christianity and other-than-Christian diversity – they would be found along the whole length of it, perhaps with more Friends clustering somewhere around the middle. The same would probably be true if Friends were asked to place themselves along the banana in relation to their

13 David Boulton, an author and broadcaster who describes himself as "a Quaker humanist", talks of how "we humans have been 're-envisioning God' ever since we came up with the god-idea" and suggests: "One way to re-envision God in the 21st century is to see him as the protagonist in our great heritage of God-stories. This God is our human creation, our imaginative fiction." David Boulton, ed., *Godless for God's Sake* (Dent: Dales Historical Monographs, 2006), pp.11–12.

belief in or experience of God. Those Quakers with a strong belief in the traditional God of the Bible would place themselves at one end, and another minority who are certain they have no need or sense of God at the other. Everyone else would find a place somewhere along the banana spectrum, reflecting how our understandings about God are invariably complex. David Rush, an American Friend and author of *They Too Are Quakers: A survey of 199 nontheist Friends*, writes of various British and American surveys of belief: "One very important gap in knowledge concerns what Quakers mean when they speak of God, quite apart from the question of belief. This writer senses that the theist/non-theist divide is far more fluid than we have supposed, and that we will find this divide often to be a false one."[14]

It is also worth bearing in mind Karen Armstrong's point that at an early stage of their history Jews, Christians and Muslims were all called atheists by their contemporaries, "because their conception of the divine was so radically different from current notions as to seem blasphemous."[15] Something of this same fear of revolutionary change is being experienced today in local meetings when Friends express concern about whether the silence of Quaker worship is actually masking real differences in people's understanding of what they are doing as they sit together. This discomfort is amplified when some Friends question whether Quakers should even use the term "worship", given the theology it implies[16].

In his pamphlet *Finding the Words: Quaker experience and language*[17], Quaker author and peace activist John Lampen attempts to discover a common language that does justice to the diversity of belief and understanding in this time of transition for British Friends. Addressing the language we use as a potential source of conflict he reminds us that "Those who reject the word

14 David Rush, "Facts and Figures", in David Boulton, ed., *Godless for God's Sake.*

15 Karen Armstrong, "God and the future", in Don Cupitt et al., *Time & Tide: Sea of Faith beyond the millennium* (Winchester: O Books, 2001).

16 See, for instance, David Boulton, "Meeting for 'weorthscipe'?", *The Friend*, 5 June 2009, p.7.

17 Published privately: copies available from 21 Heathfield Gardens, Stourbridge DY8 3YD.

"God" may not be rejecting the unnameable but the centuries of theological baggage which the word carries." He speaks of there being "something more in reality than whatever we can perceive with our senses and measure or hold in our minds", and of that "something more" being "essentially indescribable". Yet nor is this something merely the object of belief: "it is experienced by the individual as a presence – and an absence. Some of us experience it as an encounter with something personal. It is not simply an individual experience since we can also meet it as a group." Throughout their history, John Lampen points out, Quakers have maintained that everyone has the potential for this unmediated knowing. It is this direct encounter of the Other, he suggests, that has been given such names as God, The Light, The Tao, The Inward Christ, The Spirit, and That of God in everyone. What he rightly emphasises is that it is not the name we use that is important but the practical knowledge of something that happens to us. "The heart of worship is the desire and attempt to experience this presence."

Quakers, in fact, are notably pragmatic about their theology; they accept that what they are dealing with will forever remain beyond words and concepts. On the whole, British Friends at the start of the twenty-first century are comfortable to treat any imagery of God as metaphoric. They focus on the experience beneath and beyond all symbols. When Tim and I gave our presentations to the groups we worked with, many Friends resonated with these words of Dag Hammarskjöld[18], the former U.N. Secretary-General: "God does not die on the day we cease to believe in a personal deity, but we die on the day our lives cease to be illuminated by that steady radiance, renewed daily, of a wonder, the source of which is beyond all reason." And in another of the essays in *Godless for God's Sake* James Riemermann[19] expresses a view with which many Friends will identify:

> It's not a matter of simply replacing the word God with another phrase (the Divine, the Inward Light, the Christ Within, Love, the Ground of Being) but of taking all the language at my command and struggling to express how

18 Dag Hammarskjöld, *Markings* (London: Faber & Faber, 1966), p.64.
19 James Riemermann, "Mystery: It's what we don't know", in David Boulton, ed., *Godless for God's Sake*.

the world seems to me. Even then I come up short; the words rarely if ever capture the experience, but they come far closer than any timeworn, hand-me-down phrase that is likely to mean a thousand different things to a thousand different people. When the most thoughtful believers speak to me of God, it almost always comes through to me as a heightened awareness of relationship.

The American Friend Patricia Loring has described Quakerism as "a listening spirituality"; what matters most is the discipline of listening itself, the shared commitment to a process of self-surrender, to the self-forgetting and service to others that is at the heart of all spiritual practice. It is this common commitment to the surrendered life that unifies such a spiritually diverse community as British Quakers; it is Friends' willingness to lay aside personal wants and preferences and allow themselves to be led individually and collectively that draws them into unity. This deep listening for guidance is itself an expression of faith, of trust in the rightness of what will emerge when Friends "are truly listening together and to each other."[20]

Faith in transition

A recurring theme, eventually giving rise to the title of the second stage of our work with meetings or on residential events, was "Faith in Transition". The more Tim and I worked with it, the more resonance this deliberately ambiguous phrase acquired for us. On the one hand, traditional religious faith is now in question for many as their perspectives broaden with greater awareness of other ways of pursuing a spiritual path. On the other hand, for the Quaker community there is a need in such a time of change to trust, to have faith in the process of transition itself.

"Faith" has commonly been used in the religious sense of unquestioning acceptance of doctrines or articles of belief. To have faith is to believe in – as in "having faith *in* Jesus". At a deeper level, to have faith means to live in trust, to have confidence in something more profound and dependable than our everyday sense of self. Buddhist teacher Sharon Salzberg writes of this distinction: "While beliefs come to us from outside – from

20 *Quaker Faith & Practice* 3.02.

another person or a tradition or heritage – faith comes from within, from our active participation in the process of discovery." Faith, she suggests, is "the capacity of the heart that allows us to draw close to the present and find there the underlying thread connecting the moment's experience to the fabric of all life. It opens us to a bigger sense of who we are and what we are capable of doing."[21]

Faith in this sense implies action – it is a capacity of the heart that we choose to act upon. This is the faith Charles Carter refers to in his 1971 Swarthmore Lecture: "True faith is not assurance, but the readiness to go forward experimentally, without assurance. It is a sensitivity to things not yet known". Carter went on to say that Quakerism should not claim to be a religion of certainty but of uncertainty, that this is what gives Friends their special affinity with the world of science. "For what we apprehend of truth is limited and partial, and experience may set it all in a new light; if we too easily satisfy our urge for security by claiming that we have found certainty, we shall no longer be sensitive to new experiences of truth."[22] Quakers have moved a long way, especially in the last half-century, from equating faith with religious assurance. Charles Carter's words also point to a particular feature of present-day liberal British Quakerism. In a recent publication Ben Pink Dandelion argues that developments in British Quakerism in the twentieth century led to "a particular approach to theologising". Liberal Quakerism is now held together, he suggests, by *how* it believes, by a common assumption that "the group cannot know Truth, except personally, partially, or provisionally".[23] This insight reveals how firmly most British Quakers embrace the postmodern rejection of any grand unifying narrative, the contemporary proposition that there cannot be one immutable truth for all times, conditions, peoples and places.

However, there is a major challenge to the Yearly Meeting arising directly out of this acceptance of a postmodern perspec-

21 Sharon Salzberg, *Faith: Trusting your own deepest experience* (London: Element/HarperCollins, 2002).

22 Charles Carter, *On Having a Sense of All Conditions* (London: Friends Home Service Committee, 1971), p.25; quoted in *Quaker Faith & Practice* 26.39.

23 Ben Pink Dandelion, *The Quakers: A very short introduction* (Oxford: Oxford University Press, 2008), p.83.

tive: how does a community preserve enough of a common identity while respecting and being responsive to individual experience and guidance? Quakers throughout their history have achieved this, thanks in large part to the organisational genius of George Fox, who instituted a foundational structure to the Religious Society of Friends that balanced corporate discipline with the freedom of inspiration. Fox not only recognised that the Spirit may move through any individual or part of the corporate body, but also that these personal leadings must be subject to a collective testing. It is this that has kept the organisation dynamic yet stable.

Today the equilibrium of British Friends may well falter as we struggle to find true unity in the face of growing spiritual diversity. I would argue that unless Friends consciously articulate what it is that unites them today, in a way which does justice to Friends' historic Christian roots but which is no longer based on the assumption of a common Christian identity, then our contemporary pluralist Quakerism is likely to fragment. Whilst I take Ben Pink Dandelion's point about the limitations on knowing Truth as a healthy antidote to any attempt to impose an orthodoxy on others, I see, as he certainly does, an equal but opposite danger. A personal and provisional Quakerism could end up in a mire of spiritual individualism, with each person believing what they like, and with Friends no longer accountable to one another for their common faith or corporate witness.

Spiritual diversity is clearly now a fact of life for Britain Yearly Meeting and the genie cannot be put back in the bottle. Yet *something* holds us together in our different theologies and worldviews. In seeking a way forward in our diversity we can draw reassurance from recognising that while faith statements are always embedded in personal histories, Quakers collectively continue to bear witness to a corporate form of faithfulness. Our history speaks of a community being guided, testing leadings, and collectively discerning the right path. It is a premise of this book that Quakers in Britain will move to a whole new level of faith – with potentially powerful new forms of witness arising from it – as we explore more openly and articulate more publicly what that something is.

Chapter 6

Affirming Quaker commitment

Timothy Ashworth

In view of the lively diversity of contemporary spiritual practice described in the last chapter, it is not surprising that Friends today are ambivalent about placing a "boundary" around the Quaker community. Fear of excluding the very people who would benefit most from what Friends have to offer means that the line between insider and outsider in relation to a Quaker community is very weakly drawn; some would ask whether there should even be a line at all.

This is in sharp contrast to the great majority of mainstream churches. When I first went to church as an adult, despite the warm welcome, I was very clear I was on the outside of the community, and that on each occasion I attended I was being faced with a challenge over where I stood. Being a member of the church was marked by an explicit outward expression of commitment: at almost all the services, people would be invited to share the bread and wine representing the body and blood of Jesus. The teaching and meaning expressed in the repetition of this ritual vividly posed the question: do you unite yourself with the community that makes this affirmation about God and Jesus and humankind?

My first experience of a Quaker meeting for worship was very different. On entering the meeting room on that first occasion, apart from being greeted by someone at the door, there were no obvious signs of differing degrees of commitment or involvement among the seated circle of worshippers. Words spoken in the meeting indicated that the speaker was likely to have some experience of meeting for worship, and I assumed that the person who stood to give the notices at the end of worship was also fully involved in the community. But there was nothing to tell whether either of these people had more important roles than those making tea and coffee after meeting.

It was not always like this among Friends. In the earliest days and for much of Quaker history there was a great deal more awareness of the distinction between the insider and the outsider. When Friends were under threat, such a distinction mattered greatly. If the fact of being a Quaker brought with it a potential cost, whether material or social, then members of the Quaker community had a responsibility as well as a desire to mark themselves out. They did this in various ways including the language they used and their manner of dress and ways of behaving.

Today for many Friends such clarity about insider and outsider is not attractive: it goes against what most Quakers regard as a central tenet of Quaker life, its lack of exclusivity. The notice board outside the Quaker meeting I attend says: "Quakers are people of differing beliefs, lifestyles and social backgrounds. What we have in common is an acceptance that all people are on a spiritual journey. We hope we are indeed a real society of Friends, open to the world and welcoming everyone." The openness and inclusivity of the meeting is a central part of what is offered to the world outside, partly to encourage people to come and to make them feel welcome, but more importantly as an expression of Friends' testimony to equality. For some Friends who have had negative experiences of church life, this inclusivity contrasts positively with their own experience of church. As became clear to us through the work of the project, there are many Friends who have collided with the boundary walls of the Christian Church and still bear the bruises.

My own position on the issue of religious community boundaries is much more ambivalent. I have positive memories of my journey into the Catholic Church and the demands and questions the process made and asked of me. In the first place, just deciding to attend raised important questions. As I described in Chapter 1, before very long, having been surprised at what I had found in the church and drawn to investigate more, I had questions I wanted to ask of someone who could provide clear answers. It was easy to ring up the priest and say, can I come and see you? My questions were already focusing on the requirements of being a

Catholic Christian: what is essential; what is peripheral? How do I explore the Catholic faith and understand it better? As well as the books he gave me to read, the priest encouraged me to work with a group that had been involved for many years in providing friendly, practical support for some of the struggling members of the parish. At every stage I was being effectively inducted into the community. The more I learnt, the more I found myself making small assents to what I was encountering, all of which prepared me for saying "yes" when it was clear that becoming a member of the church was my next step.

The value of commitment

I can see the attraction of inclusivity and, indeed, have benefited hugely in my own life from the welcome I have received from Friends. I can also appreciate the distrust so many feel about exclusivity, with its implicit sense of superiority over others. But I also know the value of what I experienced as wholly positive and deepening about the journey into commitment I was required to make in order to join the Catholic Church – a community that, for all its size, still maintains clear boundaries concerning the essentials necessary for membership.

Perhaps especially valuable was the acceptance of a particular discipline of life, an authoritative framework that provided clarity about what was most helpful and what might hinder in this life I was coming to value. In accepting the fundamental goodness of this particular "way", I was accepting a tradition that laid certain things before me and said: it is worth your while to give these your attention. I was accepting that I was entering a community with a long established and shared wisdom on the fundamentals of Catholic faith. Although I could not always see why some things were regarded as important in the tradition, I accepted that they were valued for a purpose, had been tested over many generations and were worth my attention now. It was the lived experience of the church that drew me; once I had felt that attraction, acceptance of a certain discipline and a willing exploration of the tradition followed.

I found that the process of being drawn to one particular path, walking step by step down it and eventually accepting it, led to a deepening change of perspective. A telling observation Alex made in the course of one of our project events helpfully illuminates the relationship between this process and the issue of exclusivity. He said that in trying to make sense of exclusive religious truth claims he had recognised the language used to express these claims as the language of love. The quality of permanent faithful religious exclusivity replicates the language of the lover for the beloved: "Forsaking all others, keep thee only unto him or her, so long as ye both shall live", say the traditional marriage vows. And the analogy is a serious one. While the commitment of marriage proves difficult for so many, behind the value placed on it is the sense that this unreserved and total commitment to just one person, even as it closes down the possibility of other relationships, opens up a richness of life not realisable without the commitment. In the same way, it was my experience that the steps I took towards an exclusive commitment to God in the Christian church, a commitment without reservation, opened up possibilities not available to me without it.

During the project, Alex often made the legitimate point that, in relation to the strength and depth of the Christian tradition, the newer forms of religious and spiritual seeking can seem woolly and insubstantial. The Christian tradition has two millennia of history and experience to draw on and clearly cannot be compared to the diverse range of groups and movements that emerged from the social and religious turning point of the 1960s. These influences on contemporary spirituality also include insights and practices coming from ancient and neglected traditions of the past, and from other religious traditions that are now an integral part of our multicultural society. While these traditions certainly do not lack depth, they have not previously had so much prominence in the West and are often approached by spiritual seekers as availably new, alternative and lacking in boundaries.

A key feature the churches and other movements grouped under the heading "Christian tradition" have in common is an agreement on certain ways of describing what they believe. Central to the Christian tradition has been a credal understanding of faith. Certain ideas are expressed in creeds – collections of distilled phrases whose purpose is to capture the collective beliefs of the Christian community: "I believe in God"; "I believe in the Holy Spirit, the holy catholic church, the communion of saints" … The largest section of sayings refers to Jesus, and to the church's established position on who he was. These creeds still provide a framework for learning what it means to be a Christian; they mark the entry point and boundary of the Christian church. Christian "catechesis" or education involves studying the creeds in order to be able to affirm them before being baptised and received into the church. At the baptism of infants, the service includes asking parents and godparents three questions based on the creed to ensure they can affirm the creeds and will bring up the child to understand these things. It is important to acknowledge that any church will teach how growing up in the knowledge of the creeds must also include acting in ways that follow from them. Although the creeds say very little about the way Jesus lived and what he taught, his example as recorded in the Gospels is implicitly present, and therefore central to the credal basis of Christian faith.

A question Friends might well consider is whether there are things for the Quaker community to learn from the way the Church teaches new members. Without compromising Friends' wariness of anything that tries to capture the subtlety of faith in a fixed from of words, there may yet be value in drawing on elements of the ways other faith communities help establish a sense of commitment.

Quaker commitment

One of the first things I was given by the Catholic priest I visited early on was the Catechism, the traditional question and answer form of presenting the teachings of the church. This little booklet included answers that will be familiar to all Catholics over a certain age: "Q: Who made you? A: God made me. Q: Why did God make you? A: God made me to know Him, love Him and serve Him in this world, and to be happy with Him for ever in the next." A long section of the Catechism addresses "The Commandments". It talks of "obedience", detailing what is forbidden and providing helpful examples for some of the obscure words. A further lengthy section on the creed includes a sequence of questions about each of the "articles".

When people who are unfamiliar with the Quaker tradition start attending meeting, they will often be given a similar pocket-sized book. Reading *Advices & Queries* is a relatively easy way for the newcomer to grasp the essentials of Quaker faith. The similarity does not stop there. *Advices & Queries* also contains a long numbered list of short sections in memorably pithy phrases.

But the differences between these two booklets are substantial and crucial. It would be easy to elaborate on these differences in ways that would support a caricature of the Catholic faith, particularly as the copy of the Catechism I was given was published in 1933. While respecting the integrity of each tradition, it is illuminating to examine the ways in which *Advices & Queries* transmits the Quaker faith, in contrast to the way the Catechism does this for the Catholic faith.

The whole structure of *Advices & Queries* – the way it is written, its tone, the way the wisdom it contains is placed in front of the reader – is diametrically opposed to a credal expression of religious wisdom. Do the advices and queries carry authority? Most certainly. Do they convey tried and tested wisdom? Without a doubt. Is the subject matter religious? Evidently it is. But the form the booklet takes is precisely expressed in its title. It is a collection of bits of advice based upon the experience of the Quaker community, and questions for individuals and communities to ask themselves. And just as effectively as the creed does, it places things of importance in front of readers with the implication that it is worth their while to note and reflect on them. "Take heed", the opening words of the first query, accurately expresses the purpose of the whole document: selfishness, habit, lethargy may have blinded you to what is important; this set of questions and advice will counter that by asking you to pay careful attention to what Friends down the generations have found to be things that matter. There is here, most certainly, a Quaker tradition, a shared wisdom that can be passed on.

A further comparison between the two traditions is perhaps more challenging to Friends. When someone unfamiliar with Friends decides to come to meeting for worship they can hardly mistake the meeting for a Catholic mass. But they would be wrong to assume that the simplicity of meeting for worship is an indication of a more comprehensible or transparent environment. Despite my meeting's notice board, there is an exclusivity about Quaker worship. If ten people were drawn at random from the buses on the busy road going past the meeting house and placed in meeting for worship without any preparation, however warm the welcome, they would feel as much at sea as a similar group placed in the middle of a Catholic mass. Anyone coming across a copy of the Catholic Catechism for the first time might well be mystified, probably amused and quite possibly annoyed by it. The same person picking up *Advices & Queries* is less likely to be stirred in this way; but are they more likely to comprehend the tradition and ways of expressing it offered there? Similarly, someone wandering into mass will probably not remain emotionally neutral about what they find; the experience of wandering into a Quaker meeting may be less charged, but does that mean it is, in fact, more welcoming? It may just be that a tradition and practice less provoking of reaction is simply easier to ignore – and less easy to feel part of.

In just about the last project event Alex and I led at Woodbrooke, one of the participants, challenged by the metaphor of the skin of the banana in the model to define the boundary of Quaker identity, said that in the end it may come down to a commitment to meeting for worship. Most Friends would recognise this particular form of worship and decision-making as expressing the heart of Quaker life. While it is true that adopting a creed or accepting a set of precepts is not necessary in order to participate in meeting for worship, accepting some significant features of Quaker practice is essential. Worshippers need to be reasonably comfortable with the silence, to have a sense of receptivity, to be able to let go of personal preoccupations, and to find within themselves an openness to quite subtle and undemonstrative expressions of religious faith.

These requirements are even more essential when the meeting is a meeting for worship for business with the task of making decisions. These meetings depend on a willingness to accept a set of disciplines in which things are said and points made without any of the normal cut and thrust of discussion and argument. This disciplined form of interaction, which is inextricably linked with the meeting for worship, runs against the grain for most people. Even though in their application Quaker practices are gentle and non-confrontational, they are disciplines nonetheless and, like the more obvious rituals of the Catholic Church, are caught as much as taught.

Quakers are wary of speaking about beliefs that unite the community. Acknowledging instead the centrality of meeting for worship in Quaker faith leads Friends to place at the heart of the life of the community the experience of being "led" or "prompted" to speak or to act. The Quaker way of worship also provides a framework in which those leadings or promptings can be tested and supported by the whole community. Those who accept the Quaker way are necessarily accepting this discipline of worship and decision-making. Can someone who does not appreciate or understand this discipline really unite themselves with Friends? And, if not, is this exclusivity a bad thing? Or is it the necessary reality of being a particular community of people who over a good many generations have accepted the wisdom of living a certain way?

Commitment without creeds

Reflecting on how I have been drawn to and continue to be attracted to the Quaker way of expressing the religious life, I am very aware of what keeps me within the boundaries of the Quaker community. This can be put very simply in few words, even though they describe something profoundly important to me: I value above all the continued confidence, shared by the Quaker community, that it is possible to discern and act upon the living word of God.

This is an extraordinary perception about the nature of God, which is affirmed at every Quaker meeting. And the affirmation remains true even if we are more comfortable using the word Spirit instead of God. Such a God has to be concerned with the detail of our lives – individually and communally. This was the experience of God that overwhelmed me after my encounter with Andrew Cohen. The affirmation that, like every Christian, I had made in faith – that God counts every hair of our heads – became vividly real. I sensed God as present in every step of my life; and knew that the most extraordinary freedom could co-exist with being carefully guided and intimately cared for. This experience of God was clearly present for early Friends, and Quakers today speak of the same thing:

> In our meetings for worship we seek through the still-
> ness to know God's will for ourselves and for the gath-
> ered group. Our meetings for church affairs, in which
> we conduct our business, are also meetings for worship
> based in silence, and they carry the same expectation that
> God's guidance can be discerned if we are truly listening

together and to each other ... We have a common purpose in seeking God's will through waiting and listening, believing that every activity of life should be subject to divine guidance. (*Quaker Faith & Practice* 3.02)

When I first joined Friends for meeting for worship, and especially meeting for worship for business, I was aware of stepping into a tradition of faith that recognised and validated my experience and was absolutely in line with my growing Christian commitment over many years.

In the later stages of weekends when Alex and I were working with groups of Friends, the focus often moved to the question of what unites Friends with different perceptions of God and the Christian tradition. From our different perspectives Alex and I were both able to affirm the importance for Quakers of a "listening spirituality". This picks up on the title of a two-volume work by Patricia Loring[1], an American Quaker who has gathered spiritual practices together from different traditions in which listening to the Spirit and listening to each other are central disciplines. Alex and I found, over many years of encouraging a deepening dialogue when working together with groups, that people were keen to discuss this fundamental Quaker practice. What is more, they could do so without tripping up immediately on different ideas concerning the question of who or what is being listened to. This question is not irrelevant, yet deeper answers can be gained from first entering into the practice of listening before turning to the theological questions arising from the experience.

In this aim we were aware of connecting with the Quaker understanding of worship as being concerned with discovering the place where words arise, as expressed in this famous quotation from Isaac Penington about the purpose or "end" of words: "And the end of words is to bring men to the knowledge of things beyond what words can utter" (*Quaker Faith & Practice* 27.27).

George Fox said that "the intent of all speaking is to bring into the life" (*Quaker Faith & Practice* 2.73). Some of the most controversial things that were said by Fox and other early Friends came from their understanding of Paul's words on how the letter could not give life (2 Cor 3:6). For them, all scripture, including the Gospels, was contained in this view. Without the life that the

1 Patricia Loring, *Listening Spirituality*, 2 vols (Washington Grove, MD: Openings Press, 1997).

scriptures arose from, the words were "dust" and just a "husk".

These early Friends described themselves as "publishers" or "witnesses of the truth" but were absolutely clear that "the truth" could not be captured in word or ritual, no matter how clever or holy. Words can point to the truth but can never contain it. This is simple to state but has far reaching consequences; it implies being open to expressions of the truth arising from outside Quakerism and Christianity, for example in other faith traditions and from the diverse influences expressed loosely as "other-than-Christian" in the model. If words cannot reliably carry the truth, they cannot act as adequate boundary markers, nor can they provide a definition of the truth by which individuals can judge or be judged. Here is an important basis for Friends suspicion of creeds.

As someone who has approached Friends with a very positive view of the Christian tradition, I would also want to affirm something that was clearly stated by early Friends but which, in these more restrained and ecumenical times, Friends tend to be shy about. This view of creeds as unnecessary for holding or protecting the truth has a further consequence. A particular kind of dependence upon the words of the creed, and indeed other forms of word and ritual within the Christian tradition, can too easily become a block to realising the truth they are meant to convey. While religious forms can reveal deeper truths, they may also trap people in understandings that make depth more difficult to find and to explore. And this fact is compounded by how such forms come to define the community. The way that faith is bound up with belonging to a particular community means that questioning the forms can be seen as a threat to faith. There tends to be an over-investment in the particular forms that make a community distinct, which mark out its boundary. It is worth acknowledging that Friends are not immune to this process! An absence of ritual forms may be a defining marker of Quaker practice, but insisting on their absence for that reason becomes a form in itself, which may similarly block Friends from finding the depth they seek.

To put this in the context of "the faith of Jesus" as explained in Chapter 4, in order to discover the same living faith Jesus had in God it is necessary to let go of faith in forms, whether these forms are the rituals of baptism and eucharist, creeds or other forms of words, or even hallowed bits of scripture. Where faith is perceived of as holding on to something fixed and reliable, the very act of holding on prevents the letting go necessary for encountering God's Spirit – which is not to be pinned down.

Perhaps we can see from this why ambivalence about the Christian tradition, from which Quaker faith has grown, is so deeply rooted in the Quaker tradition. On the one hand, the Christian tradition, with its prophetic understanding of the relationship between humankind and God, is deeply affirmed by Quaker experience. On the other, the way this tradition has been passed down through words and rituals, which have themselves come to be regarded as sacred, blocks the ability to gain direct access to the very things they seek to define.

Earlier, I affirmed that what I most value about the Quaker way is the continued confidence, shared by the Quaker community, that it is possible to discern and act upon the living word of God. Here, I would like to expand on that by being more explicit about the importance I place on the Christian roots of Quakerism by adding and emphasising (in italics) two phrases. I feel I belong within the Quaker boundary because of a continued confidence, shared by the community, that it is possible, *through tried and tested ways of worshipping and listening together,* to discern and act upon the living word of God, *the same living word that spoke in and acted through Jesus.* The life of the Church witnesses to God at work in Jesus, and I find I still need the Church to keep placing in front of me stories and interpretations of Jesus that continue to stretch my understanding and shape my life. Yet, Quaker experience over three and a half centuries shows clearly that the discernment of God's living word, and the clarity and courage to follow it, does not need the ritual and hierarchical framework of the Church. Indeed, when faith in God is confused with faith in word and ritual, they become obstacles to hearing the living word spoken now.

It is Friends' tried and tested ways of worshipping and listening together that mark out the Quaker community, and which provide a framework for corporate faith and action. These essential practices have shaped and framed the Quaker community over generations. They can still bring clarity today to the question of how the distinctive Quaker tradition is passed on to others, so they can grow to make their own commitment to it.

Chapter 7
Revealing worship

Timothy Ashworth

In order to discover what individuals or communities believe, we can learn a lot by looking at the way they worship, and even though Quaker meeting has none of the rich symbolism of most religious rituals, the principle still applies.

Unlike many people who have come to Friends, I would number some of my experiences of Christian worship as among the most important moments of my life. They have been powerful expressions of community, involving a deep engagement of head and heart – at times for joyful celebration, at others for facing difficulty and weakness. These occasions when I have joined with others in my community to give praise and thanks to God without reservation are readily definable as worship. Quaker meeting for worship is a very different kind of experience, but there are parallels. I especially value times when I am aware of a deep sense of community, when the worshipping group has felt "gathered". Although in Quaker meeting for worship I miss the intellectual challenge and poetic richness of words of scripture and ritual, I am, from time to time, moved to tears by heartfelt ministry that emerges spontaneously and catches the present movement of the Spirit.

For me, the focus in Quaker meeting for worship is very clearly in the midst of the community. The object of worship is not *outside* or *other*. It is true that more conventional Christian worship can carry this meaning too. Christian theology speaks of God's Spirit as being the active player in prayer and worship. The community, as much as the reading of scripture or the bread and wine of the sacrament, is understood as "the presence of Christ". But so much of the drama of traditional

Christian worship places the attention outside the individual or community. Does the Catholic who, when leaving church, genuflects towards the tabernacle containing what for him or her is the consecrated body of Christ, also feel the same devotion and respect for all the other individuals who themselves – in Catholic understanding – carry this same presence within them? The power and specialness of Catholic worship tends to overwhelm the very purpose it seeks to effect – the recognition of and response to the presence of God in the whole of life.

The Quaker community is founded upon an experience in which the service of God, the worship of God, is the whole of a life led in God's Spirit. It seems to me that a *meeting* for worship is really the gathering together at an agreed time to do, in a certain way, what everyone is doing in their own way all the time. All life is Spirit-filled. All of life is the worship. And, from time to time, the community "meets" to join together for this in a particularly clear and explicit way, and sometimes "meets" to do business. The worship does not start and stop when the community gathers and departs.

In that time for "meeting" there is little to look at other than the people present, but that itself is a powerful sign. All are full and equal participants in the act of worship. Each person has a priestly role; anyone at any time may feel called to speak and everyone in the gathered group needs to listen. With no sanctuary set apart for especially sacred actions, it is very clear that the community itself is the heart of the drama.

Arguably, the questions that regularly emerge within the Quaker community over what or who is being worshipped arise from the specific way in which Quaker worship is conducted. When the focus is so strongly placed in the midst of the community, that makes it difficult to sustain the traditional Christian categories in which God is often referred to as "other" and, at times, awesomely "Other". While in the Quaker tradition it is common to speak of waiting upon God's guidance, the Quaker way of worship encourages a perception of God as present and accessible – to each of us and as a gathered group, directly and at all times. Quaker ways make it less easy to make the mistake of thinking that when God is spoken of as personal and as "guiding", this means God is somehow apart from us, separate from the community or the individual.

Worship and the reign of God

The Quaker tradition has helped me explore a particular under-standing of the kingdom or reign of God. Quaker worship is typified by an absence of the symbols that many churches use to signify the presence of God, but there is nevertheless, in the ideas of "waiting" and "guidance", an indicator of something to wait for and from which guidance will come.

While the powerful sense of being led to speak comes to an individual, the whole community carries a commitment to this understanding of "leading" as not simply personal but as a real activity of the Spirit in the community. By implication, behind the Quaker openness to guidance in worship and in everyday life is the confidence that there is a direction to this guidance, not just for individuals but also for the community.

The traditional Christian understanding sees this direc-tion as being towards the realisation of "the reign of God" on earth. One of the things that has been a real revelation for me in understanding more about Friends is an expanded way of seeing the reign of God as fundamentally about the establishment of a new order in humankind. The early Friends, full of apocalyptic visions as they were, did not see the reign of God as a cataclysmic intervention from outside in which, to take one example, the earth is physically consumed by fire before a new world comes to birth. Rather, they saw it as a dramatic upheaval in the human heart in which a limited self-centred perception of who we are gives way to a consciousness that is wide and free, and which rec-ognises an interconnectedness with all beings.

Not that this means that the reign of God is simply a per-sonal spiritual reality detached from issues of justice and peace, or from the conditions in which people live. Precisely the oppo-site is the case; it is when actions are done by a group in the same Spirit with which Jesus acted that the reign of God is at hand. This is zeal to reform the world not based on ideology but, as has been shown repeatedly by effective reforming Quaker action, motivated by a present experience of the Spirit, the same Spirit of sturdy and challenging compassion as was in Jesus.

Where my Christian faith also leads me, and where not all Friends will want to go, is to the conviction that the reign of God that Jesus spoke of is not simply a series of dramatic momentary glimpses or an inspiring vision, but a real transformation yet to come. Partly influenced by Quaker worship and practice, I have come to see the reign of God as human transformation, as establishing a new way of being and acting together in all humankind. This is not to say, as I know Alex fears, that the Christian understanding is about human domination over creation but, rather, owning our God-given place in it, free from selfishness, able to participate creatively in God's love for all that is. This is what "made in the image of God" really means. This, it seems to me, is what early Friends had tasted and what gave them the sense that the world was being transformed. As they put it, "Christ has come to teach his people himself"; the same power that was in Christ is available to all to effect real change.

Meeting for worship for business

Quaker silent worship, with its occasional words of ministry offered by anyone present and taking place in simple surroundings with absence of ritual, does indeed tell us a lot about the Quaker way and where Friends' spiritual priorities lie. But it doesn't give us the whole picture. To really understand what underpins Quaker spiritual practice we need to look at how Friends conduct their business meetings, properly called meetings for worship for business. This unusual method of corporate decision-making is a Quaker practice that both emphasises and depends on an understanding of diversity, of the value of each person in creating the community and the activities it takes forward.

When the American Jesuit Michael Sheeran produced his study on Friends' ways of making decisions, *Beyond Majority Rule*,[1] he described how, as part of the renewal of the Catholic Church in the last century, each religious community was invited to return to its roots. The Jesuits looked back into their history and discovered a forgotten decision-making procedure called "Communal Discernment". When efforts were made to implement this practice they found constant obstacles to success. In particular, Michael Sheeran says, "lack of acceptance of the process, mistrust of other participants, and inability to put aside one's own interests" habitually blocked the process. It was through look-

1 *Beyond Majority Rule: Voteless decisions in the Religious Society of Friends* (Philadelphia: Philadelphia Yearly Meeting, 1983),

ing for other communities that had day-to-day experience of this method that Michael Sheeran turned to Friends, as he puts it, "a small religious family of some two hundred thousand members worldwide who have utilized Communal Discernment – without using the name – as their ordinary decision-making process for the past three centuries" (p.xiii). His sense of the centrality of this practice to Christian life is unreserved. "… Friends successfully employ a tradition of religious decision-making which is deeply embedded in Scripture but which other Christians have typically lost" (p.xiii–xiv).

Where that tradition of religious decision-making receives strong scriptural support is in a section of one of Paul's letters. In the course of 1 Corinthians 12–14 he uses the famous image of the body and its members as a way of illuminating the inter-relationship of the various parts of a Christian community. In this whole passage Paul is exploring how to order a community that understands itself as Spirit-led, as prophetic. He starts by affirming how in this community the living God is speaking, unlike the dumb idols of the past. Towards the end of the section, we find the verses already referred to in Chapter 4 where Paul explains how a gathering is to be ordered whereby each person who is given words for the community speaks in turn, "so that all may learn and all be encouraged" (in the building of the community). When I point this section out to Quakers, they recognise it immediately as a description of how vocal ministry happens in Quaker worship today. Indeed, the Quaker community has had three and a half centuries of being an "experimental" faith, of trying to live as a prophetic community, open to the Spirit in every aspect of community life.

It is in this context of the experience of the Spirit-led life that Paul looks at diversity within a community. While there are many different tasks and skills, he says, there is one Spirit operating through all of them. All of them are needed. All need each other. Quakers have found that it is possible to stay true to the fundamental principle Paul presents but to expand its consequences given the greater knowledge that we have now. In this book, we have largely focused on the wide range of religious and spiritual experiences that different individuals now bring into the Quaker community. But other dimensions of diversity also influence the spiritual life of the community. Friends have embraced the insights and active ministry of both women and men in the community from the beginning. Children and young people are introduced to Quaker ways of decision-making as soon as possible and are enabled to contribute from their own perspective. Gay people are active in local and national Quaker decision-making bodies without this being regarded as exceptional in any way.

Quaker ways of working make it possible to appreciate and benefit from more subtle aspects of human diversity too. Friends have long experience of a way of working together that values and therefore gains, not only diverse from points of view, but from the fact that we bring the whole of our different personalities to our discussions and the tasks arising from them. Many Friends have explored faith and spirituality in relation to our different personality types as developed in the Enneagram and Myers-Briggs personality indicator. We are much more aware today of the different personality types within any human community, making it possible to recognise and use the diverse gifts we bring into community with a greater sensitivity and responsiveness than ever before.

The formal process of Quaker decision-making in a Quaker meeting for worship for business progresses towards the production of a "minute" to capture the insight of the group as it seeks to move forward. Those with a strong vision, concern or sense of a leading on a particular matter of business before the meeting may well be the ones offering new insights, but there will be contributions too from others who see clearly the practical problems and logistical issues that need addressing. Financially alert Friends will ensure that the vision stays in touch with the resources that are available. Every member of the meeting is a participant in this process.

Members of other churches have asked me if the openness of Quaker decision-making is not simply a front for more powerful and articulate Friends getting their own way. This is not my experience. In every Quaker meeting for business I have been involved in, I have seen extremely able people with different gifts and insights willing to enter fully into this collective discipline, in which the body of those gathered seeks a real unity where each view is valued. Factions and political persuasion completely undermine the spirit that makes the method work and do not have a place in the process. This is precisely what Paul is speaking about when he asks how the eye can say to the hand "I have no need of you". "If the whole body were an eye, where would the hearing be?" (1 Cor 12:21, 17). When Paul lists the things that run counter to the Spirit-led life, self-interest and a factional mentality make up much of the list (Gal 5:20).

From decision to action

There is an important related point here that follows from this way of working. When the Jesuit Michael Sheeran studied Friends and, in particular, Quaker ways of making decisions, one of the things he noted was that because all are involved in the decision-making, because all have some sense of it being a decision that was Spirit-led, there is a very strong commitment to follow up on the decision with practical action. What this leads to is a high sense of responsibility among a worshipping Quaker group. All those engaged in the decision-making *own* the decision and their part in its implementation.

I once wrote a short piece of text for a course in which I carelessly referred in passing to Quakers as being a leaderless community. A colleague rightly picked up on this. What she said was that Friends are not a leaderless community, but one in which leadership does not get institutionally fixed upon particular individuals. As Paul presents it, leadership is just one role among the diversity of roles in the community. Paul refers to different special roles within the community: some are teachers, some administrators, some healers. Quaker experience supports this, but also confirms through the practice of triennial appointments[2] that these roles do not have to have to be permanently identified with particular individuals. The purposes of a community are well served by flexibility in the sharing and changing of roles as individuals develop their capabilities and bring freshness to newly accepted tasks.

So when a community works well, leadership can move around according to the gifts and needs within a community.

---

2 Quakers are appointed to roles usually for a three-year term (sometimes less). They may be appointed to a second term at the discretion of the meeting. In this way most Friends serve in a number of roles over a period of time.

There is no doubt that the clerk does have a leadership role in meetings for business, but this role is to do with enabling participation, making sure that all views have been heard and have shaped the decision as appropriate. Friends describe the role of clerk as the "servant of the meeting", reflecting a very different attitude to leadership and leaders in the Quaker community. It is not easy to attack those in leadership roles when they are so clearly fellow members of the community, when the tasks they undertake on behalf of the meeting will have been experienced by others in the group, and might well be the future experience of anyone else. This Quaker view of serving the meeting through the sharing of roles further strengthens the collective sense of responsibility for the worship, work and witness of the meeting community.

And a Quaker meeting is shaped not only by this explicit approach to the sharing of leadership and other roles, but also by each new person who attends the meeting. While this will vary depending upon the liveliness of a meeting, any new member can move quickly into playing a part in the community into which they come, bringing their own story and particular gifts evolved through their own experience. Friends certainly have a strong tradition to pass on to newcomers and succeeding generations, but the Quaker community has ways of valuing the inspirations and traditions of the past without allowing them to overwhelm or limit inspirations arising in the present. This is why *Quaker Faith & Practice*, the anthology of writings on Quaker experience and guidance (see Introduction, p.8), is revised each generation. Some quotations and ways of doing things have been retained from the earliest days, but there are always new insights and new ways of organising the life of the community. This in itself is an extraordinary fact. It shows that Quakers fully embrace an understanding of how the Spirit is leading the community to evolve. When an earlier way of responding to a situation is seen to be inadequate in changed circumstances, or Friends recognise a need for development, there is a confidence that such new developments can be tested and then relied upon. The past has bequeathed to Friends reliable ways of working out how to test new insights and create the bridge to the future.

Quaker worship is so unlike the grand liturgies of some churches and other faiths that a degree of sensitivity is required to see how relatively undemonstrative actions in Quaker worship can reveal deeper meanings. There is something symbolic about moving the Bible and *Quaker Faith & Practice* to one side to make way for the book of minutes at a meeting for business. The minute book is not regarded with any special veneration by Friends beyond the fact that it may need to be consulted sometimes and therefore needs properly looking after. Nevertheless, it is very revealing of how Quakers understand the way inspiration works among Friends, of how God can speak in a prophetic community. In a context of worship, the wisdom and knowledge of all the individuals in the community are brought to bear upon a matter the meeting needs to attend to, out of which the clerk discerns "the sense of the meeting" and records this in the minute. It may be an internal matter for the meeting, it may be something of wider concern; in each case the clerk writes down what has been discerned and what action needs to be taken, ensuring that the meeting is able to unite around what is recorded in the minute. But despite this real sense of "inspiration", of the minute capturing something that is Spirit-led, the written record does not then become in any sense special or "holy".

Sometimes a minute does come to be read for inspiration at some future date, but much more usually it remains just a part of a whole process of inspiration going on in the present. While it is one person who writes the minute (with some help from their assistant), it is a necessarily collective task using the diverse insights of everyone present in the meeting for business. It can never be said that one Friend produced a minute, nor that the minute was solely a product of the present moment when it was written. It is the collective wisdom formed of past and present Quaker experience that shapes the minute, which in turn provides the direction towards the future. From the moment it is written, the minute is only a reference point; it only has real value in relation to the outcome it points towards. The clerk may be thanked for a skilfully written minute but an inspirational text is not the aim. The Spirit-led task is to produce a minute that gathers what the meeting has recognised as its role on the matter, in a form that enables the Meeting to move forward on it effectively. It is the whole process of discernment into action – of which the minute is certainly an important part – that is the holy task, that is holiness in action.

God's way of working

So, right at the heart of Quaker ways of working is an appreciation of diversity – of leadership, precise thinking, vision, pragmatism, financial acumen, all working together in the same group
in the context of worship. But it is more than just appreciation
of diversity that is involved. The Quaker way recognises that the
diversity within the community is a gift without which the community cannot function; the diversity of the many members is
necessary for the Spirit to operate. Friends rediscovered a way of
working that puts the living, guiding Spirit at the centre of the
community, with the group process, of both giving voice to inspiration and testing that inspiration, being essential to the leadership of the Spirit. In the everyday lives of any individual Quaker
community, staying true to both the discipline and the theology of this practice will always be something of a challenge. But
the point should not be missed. On the principle that worship
reveals what a community believes, this business method prac-
tised in a spirit of worship reveals something that is foundational,
not just to Quaker ways of doing things but also to the Quaker
understanding that must necessarily flow from this: that inspiration operating through diversity is God's way of working.

Michael Sheeran, in the conclusion to his book, contrasts
the individualistic ways of the world with a way of seeing things
based in community. It is this, he says, that makes the Quaker
approach possible and effective. In the middle of the words of
Paul we considered earlier comes his famous passage where he
says that the greatest of God's gifts is love. "Love is patient; love is
kind; love is not envious or boastful or arrogant or rude. It does
not insist on its own way; it is not irritable or resentful ..." (1 Cor
13:4–5). Here, simply expressed, are the necessary human attri-
butes for the practical and effective working of Spirit-led community. The communities formed and supported by Paul faced
the same challenges as Quaker communities today: how do we
value the insights of every individual without getting locked in
arguments and disputes? How do we combine the order a community needs with the present inspiration of the Spirit? How do
we ensure that "discipline" continues to nourish inspiration and
does not squeeze it out? The process of meeting for worship for
business can sometimes seem protracted, but it is nevertheless

an extraordinary witness to the way the Spirit leads a community into unity. This is far from some kind of divine quiz with the Spirit having the answer – which it takes a long time for a group of rather slow people to plod their way towards.

What a Quaker meeting for business affirms is that it is specifically through the diversity with which the community faithfully responds to the movement of the Spirit that an embracing and guiding unity emerges. Many Friends have experience of meetings for business in which apparently irreconcilable statements are eventually drawn together into a more rich and true insight. Every time this happens it is a joyful experience of diversity and unity that are both Spirit-led. Paul was affirming this reality at the heart of Christian community, yet so often the Christian claims concerning the leadings of the Spirit have been experienced as suppression of diversity and demand for conformity. If Michael Sheeran is right, the Quaker tradition offers tools of discernment that are not readily available elsewhere, ways of working and worshipping that mean there is nothing to fear from flexibility and diversity, so that no hierarchy or creed need restrain the living "order" of the Spirit.

Given that worship, the subject of this chapter, is central to how Friends make decisions, this distinctive and valued way of working is clearly not just a preferred method of doing things, but a belief about how things are. The diversity in humankind, and indeed in all creation, is itself a revelation of God's presence. Far from being an obstacle to the oneness that is often regarded as the goal of religious life, the diversity in a Quaker meeting is itself a celebration of God. Quaker meeting for worship for business reveals how to appreciate diversity in practice, and through this unique way of working discover how to move forward together.

Chapter 8

Naming our common ground

Alex Wildwood

When I first drew an elongated shape representing Quakerism across the final diagram of the model explained in Chapter 3, it was jokingly dubbed "the Quaker banana". But from that moment, the shape also became a metaphor – for something clearly contained inside its own skin, or boundary. This useful image prompts us to ask: what defines the skin of the Quaker banana? I hear this question reflected in a concern, expressed quite often in local meetings – including from people who are otherwise positive about Quaker diversity – that the Society is in danger of trying to be all things to all people. In other words, we need clarity about the boundary of Quakerism in the Yearly Meeting. So how do we decide where the boundary lies?

In the previous chapter, Tim described the central importance of the Quaker way of worship and of the decision-making process that grew out of this, which suggests that the boundary is more to do with the distinctive practices of Friends than either our history or any statements we make about our faith. Working on the project Tim and I often heard people say that, surely, our testimonies define what it is to be a Quaker. I find this response unsatisfactory in two ways: it is not far off having a credal basis to our faith (agree with these principles and you are one of us) and it can amount to a secularisation of something central to being Quaker. Many people of goodwill respect everyone as equal and try to live truthfully, peacefully and simply. This does not make them Quakers. My understanding of the Quaker testimonies is that they are a comparatively recent elaboration of Friends' one original testimony, which was to the presence and guidance of God. It was this experience – of convincement – that led Friends to live in a certain (ethical) way. If we make the testimonies the basis of Quaker identity, they may become an outward form taking the place of this foundational religious experience of Friends. While it is possible for Friends to subscribe to the testimonies without a clear sense of the power behind them, in doing so we lose something crucial: we are no longer making ourselves available to the guidance of a power greater than ourselves.

Early Friends spoke repeatedly of the power of God. For me the integrity of our meetings lies in our common yearning for a sense of this power, for seeking the truth in our hearts[1], discerned and tested together in prayerful stillness. It is this religious intention from which all our witness, all our actions for good, follow. Without this, we invite the error of imagining we know what the world needs and we try to put the world to rights *in our own strength*. If we lack this religious underpinning we also lose the deeply shared purpose essential for holding us together in diversity and preventing us drifting towards divergence.

Newcomers are sometimes led to understand you can believe what you like as a Quaker, which is a problematic half-truth. It is true that Quakers do not impose a belief system on anyone. When people are drawn to our way of worship and way of life, we invite them to try it for themselves and, if it suits them, to stay. But as they grow in relationship with the Quaker tradition we do them a disservice – and set up problems for future generations of Quakers – if we do not explain why we do things as we do, what our underlying beliefs are.

I think it is impossible to speak of experience without involving beliefs in some way, because we all move between belief and personal experience, or our direct inner knowing, all the time. For example, in meeting for worship, sitting in silence is based on a belief about what may happen as we wait expectantly. Vocal

1 George Fox: "Blessed be the lord, truth is reached in the hearts of people beyond words." From the American diary, 1672, in *Journal*, ed. John Nickalls (Cambridge: Cambridge University Press, 1952), p.639; quoted in Rex Ambler, *Truth of the Heart* (London: Quaker Books, 2001), p.18.

ministry is unintelligible as a religious practice unless under-stood in a belief framework of prophetic speaking, of being moved to bear witness and testify to faith in words and in actions in the world. I think that, collectively, we cannot adequately talk about – still less transmit – our faith without referring to such underlying beliefs.

Because it is many decades now since there was a majority of birthright Friends in Britain Yearly Meeting who were grounded in Quaker faith through their upbringing, we cannot assume the beliefs at the heart of the Quaker way are well understood. This is one reason I think there is now a great need in Britain Yearly Meeting for a teaching ministry to articulate and transmit what is essential to our faith and practice, and also to help Friends understand how and why these essentials exist.

In the light of the range of faith positions now existing within the Society, it is quite a challenge to attempt to define the implicit beliefs of Quakerism, but what I can offer here is my personal view. I would say they boil down to the following: As Quakers we believe that in the silence we may hear "the still small voice of God". We believe that through this we will be led to com-passionate action in the world; Friends are not a church focused on personal salvation or enlightenment but on the redemption of the world from suffering, injustice and oppression. We believe that the will of God, understood as the right way forward, the truth of a situation, will be revealed in the stillness of expectant waiting together. We believe "that of God" to be present in all people and beings and that obedience to God (listening for the truth, perceiving reality directly) leads us to live according to our testimonies, which is a way of life where truth, equality, simplicity and peace become the touchstones of personal lives and all our dealings with others – from intimate relationships to the global arena. These beliefs may be implicit in Quaker practice rather than stated explicitly, but I would say that it is on all these beliefs that Quakerism is founded.

Importantly, we do not start with beliefs as abstract princi-ples that newcomers must accept in order to join us in worship. Quaker practice invites people to explore for themselves what William Penn described as an "experiment" upon the human soul:

The whole, indeed, being but a Scriptural experiment upon the soul, and therefore seeks for no implicit credit, because it is self-evident to them that will uprightly try it.[2]

And when anyone asks Friends to explain things further, we should be able to articulate clearly the rootedness of our faith and our practice – in the Christian tradition and in the process of continuing revelation; in other words, the things underlying our faith, which we believe in. As Quakers we might emphasise the translation of beliefs into action in the world, but articulating our beliefs is also an action. We need to be able to express these core beliefs not as articles of faith but as the spiritual basis of our common practices, our working for justice, peace and the integrity of the Earth-community.

This is where I feel our rootedness in tradition is so important. While Quakers undoubtedly place great emphasis on an experiential faith, it is not just any kind of experience. Liberal Friends are fond of quoting George Fox: "What canst thou say?" not always recognising this as being far from an open invitation to state our personal opinion or to speak merely from individual experience. Fox qualified his question significantly by adding, "Art thou a child of the Light, hast walked in the Light, and what thou speakest is it inwardly from God?"[3]. My understanding of this is that Quaker experience of faith is not just each person's private inner knowing; it is experience known inwardly through being *held in the light.* Believing that the Spirit may move through any one of us, Friends certainly value each person's experience, but we draw coherence from this through our tradition of collective testing and discernment. It is the practices and ways of doing things Friends have evolved, underpinned by our implicit core beliefs, which bring unity to the community. This is quite different from basing our faith on a set of beliefs, a creed. We derive strength and purpose from our clarity on this difference, but there are inherent dangers for us too. In a time of increasing diversity in the Society, we may lose sight of the essentials of our

2 *Primitive Christianity Revived,* reprinted in: William Penn, *The Peace of Europe, the Fruits of Solitude, and other Writings,* ed. Edwin B. Bronner, (London: Everyman, 1993), p.228. I am grateful to Rex Ambler for drawing my attention to this quotation. See also p.38.

3 As reported by Margaret Fell; see *Quaker Faith & Practice* 19.07.

faith and practice if we cannot articulate, or fail to emphasise, the authentic basis of Friends' traditional ways. We are a *religious* Society and we should not be afraid to say so. I think we should be able to name what makes Friends distinctive, while still doing justice to the richness and diversity among Friends today. This is the both/and of pluralist Quakerism: the Quaker way has core implicit beliefs and overt practices, but we accommodate wide variations in how we describe the inspiration behind "the truth in our hearts" that leads us to embrace this way.

While Friends are mostly willing to accept that we choose different forms of words with a variety of shades of meaning – depending on the subtleties of our concept of God (Spirit, Light . . .) – these may not be simply different words to describe much the same thing. I am especially aware of a fundamental difference between the religious intention informing my faith and that of a Christian Quaker such as Tim, which seems to me to centre on the Christian doctrine of the nature of God. I am conscious that in referring to the divine spirit as a power greater than ourselves, this is a pale shadow of what the Christian faith has to say about the nature of God. My understanding is that for a Christian this is not just a power in an abstract way but one working in humanity towards a distinct (loving) purpose; a power engaged with each human life in an intimate way, as Tim describes. Perhaps the greatest difference between the Christian and non-Christian lies in the way we each view the direction of evolution, in other words, the aim or purpose of existence.

Tim has explained how, from his Christian perspective, he sees the reign of God as being about a new order in the human heart from which certain actions flow. I would suggest that the human heart is only one player in transforming the world. I remain critical of how strongly human-centred the Christian tradition is. In terms of humanity realising our interconnectedness with the rest of life, of "awakening to our deep ecology"[4], I find Buddhism a much more helpful starting point. In matters of faith I consider myself an "evolutionary"; I see humanity as arising from, and inextricably a part of, the entire web of existence – one manifestation of a sacred totality, an aspect of

4 I am indebted to Joanna Macy for this description of the challenge humanity faces in this time.

the emerging complexity of Life. What is special about our species is that as conscious beings, we have a particular responsibility to the whole. This is how I understand the phrase, "made in
the image of God". We have creative self-reflexive awareness, we
have the capacity to create or destroy, we have choice. But these
unique gifts do not entitle us to claim dominion over the rest.
To borrow from another tradition, we have the ability to live in
harmony with the Tao, or to fool ourselves into believing we can
survive by running counter to it. We have free will and can therefore choose freely to recognise or to deny our interdependence.
These are real theological differences between Christian and
non-Christian perspectives, not just shades of meaning attached
to our use of certain words.

Where I feel Tim and I do meet, as Christian and non-Christian, is in our experience of the power of prayer (and I believe
other non-Christian Friends might also feel they have this in
common with Friends who identify themselves as Christians).
Nevertheless, I am aware of real differences in our approaches to
prayer, especially the focus of our prayers. There is a part of me
desperately wanting to believe that what I envision as the origi-
nating Mystery, the creative, animating Presence in the universe,
can be related to in a personal way, can be conversed with – even
desires that I establish communion with Her/Him/It. Part of
me yearns for such relationship. But as soon as such yearnings
arise, the rational, sceptical voice within me judges such longing
as merely superstitious and sees it as a monstrous projection of
unfulfilled childhood needs expressed as an unhealthy tendency
towards dependency in relationships, a refusal to grow up. I am
then faced with the stark reality that there is no God *out there*
providing a safety net for humanity; that the God who intervenes
in history – or in our own lives when we beseech "Him" in the
correct way – is truly dead in this time. (And – as Nietzsche's
madman points out – it is we who have killed Him.)

This part of me educated in scientific rationalism believes
there is no prior meaning to our lives or to the universe; that
the last few hundred years of scientific exploration and discovery
have shown God as the Good Parent to be an illusion, an emotional crutch for weak and timid souls. Human beings are incar-
nations of consciousness developing neither randomly nor at
the behest of an all-powerful Deity; rather, we are the unfolding

self-realisation of a cosmic evolutionary process discovering, giving voice to, itself. Such are the conversations that as a "devout sceptic"[5] I find spin about within my head, and it is not easy to inhabit the tension between these different voices and perspectives. Yet I am also aware that when I get down on my knees and pray, something changes – though whether the change is within me, outside me, or both in and around me, I do not know.

They say there are no atheists in a life raft. I am remembering when our daughter Hannah, then aged fourteen months, was diagnosed with a particularly aggressive brain tumour and given six months to live. As she was being rushed to hospital for emergency surgery thirty miles away, I first prayed instinctively, in silence, to the all-powerful God of my childhood in whom I thought I no longer believed. At first I simply begged she might survive, that she not be taken from us. Her loss was unimaginable. Yet even within the first few hours, the way I was praying began to change. For a while I still found myself plea-bargaining with the Almighty, I prayed that she might live long enough at least for us to say goodbye, for us to be able to properly take our leave of her. We had not even had time to adjust to how seriously ill she was as we handed her over to the care of professionals who then hurried urgently about their life-saving tasks. As we waited through that first night – the longest in my life – I reached a point where my prayers changed once more. Accepting I had no control in this situation, that I was powerless over what was happening and that we were totally dependent on the skills and caring, the dedication and goodwill of complete strangers, I prayed silently, asking now for the resources to cope with the outcome – whatever that might be. For all we knew at the time, even survival might mean years of future treatment for a brain-damaged child. We faced so many uncertainties and I had no idea what we were dealing with.

As I began to relinquish control, I let go of my desire for something solid to cling on to. Groping instead for a sense of trust, desperately hoping to tap into my own wellsprings of faith, I tried to recall my personal sense of being part of something

5 The title of a BBC Radio 4 series of interviews conducted by Bel Mooney, some of which were published as a book, *Devout Sceptics: Conversations about faith and doubt* (London: Hodder & Stoughton, 2003).

so much vaster, deeper, and more mysterious than we can imagine, and to find solace in this. Under the extreme provocation of reality, I was seeking to "let go and let God", as they say in Twelve Step programmes. I may have difficulty wondering who or what I pray to but I have no doubt of the power of prayer. I know that as we were prayed for that night and in the months afterwards, the sense of being upheld by others in prayer was palpable. Some of this prayer among our friends and family (Quakers and others) would have been Christian prayer addressed to the God I find it so hard to believe exists or can influence events. But reflecting on that experience has made me realise how, when we are fuelled by what recovering addicts refer to as "the gift of desperation", even the most sceptical of us can touch into a mysterious power, which can and does transform our lives.

I also learnt from this devastating and life-changing experience that whatever differences may seem to separate us in our diverse faith positions, there is a core of human experience where – as I would describe it – we are united in the Spirit. No matter what approach we take to prayer, a point of unity can be found there. As Friends, we need to keep sight of that truth as we attempt to address the very real stumbling blocks to unity as a religious society, especially those arising from differences between us in our individual relationships with the Christian roots of Quakerism. In our work together, Tim and I both recognised that many Friends have a real difficulty with the Christian tradition, often naming as their reason horrific episodes of Christian history or the militancy of Christian evangelism. The continuing intolerance of many Christians to other faiths and wisdom traditions, the collusion of the Church with worldly powers, its sanctioning of "just" wars, its use of fear and guilt as weapons of repression, are all obvious betrayals of the example and teachings of Jesus. I know that many people who have rejected the Church, as I did, cannot take Christianity seriously without real evidence of atonement for this violent and intolerant distortion. Another difficulty with Christianity some Friends have is that, while they are comfortable with the teachings of Jesus, as modern, scientifically literate people they cannot accommodate to the medieval supernaturalism of so much of Christian faith.

These difficulties may well result in such Friends – and I count myself among them – cutting themselves off from the riches of the Christian tradition. Are we so put off by what we see as intractable dogma that we deny ourselves access to what Tim has described to me as the wonderful teachings and inspirational actions in the figure of Jesus? And, importantly from his perspective, are we rejecting the significance of what happened in the small community that sprang up after Jesus' death, which led them to say and do what they did in his name? As a faith community seeing itself as "Primitive Christianity revived", early Friends clearly modelled themselves on the early church. This is not just an interesting piece of history; it forms the basis of our commitment to immediate divine inspiration and guidance.

When a Christian today leaves another church and finds their way to Friends, it may be for much the same reasons as those Christians who heard early Friends preach and were themselves convinced or opened to a more immediate experience of the Spirit at work in their lives. Such a newcomer is turning away from aspects of the Church that no longer meet their spiritual needs, towards a very different way of experiencing the guidance of God; they nevertheless bring with them a religious grounding that helps them understand a certain amount about the Christian roots of British Friends. However, bringing their understanding of Christianity from a church background can be a mixed blessing in a Quaker meeting. While fewer people are coming to Friends through finding that doctrine, ritual forms and religious symbols get in the way of their own authentic spiritual experience, a far greater number of people coming into Friends today who have no church background, or for that matter any religious background at all. When such Friends encounter others bringing some of the certainties of a former Christian affiliation, each group may have their own misunderstanding of the distinctive nature of Quaker faith and worship.

For myself, I recognise a certain sadness in my reaction to hearing Tim describe his Christian faith. In not having that positive experience, I share something, not only with others who have negative associations with Christianity, but also with the increasing numbers of people coming into the Society for whom it has no resonance at all. Perhaps this means that as well as informing newcomers about what is distinctively Quaker, what lies within the Quaker boundary, we also need to fill in some of the Christian background. On the other hand, there are already significant numbers of British Friends who see no need to consider the Christian roots of Quakerism at all. They feel we have moved on and are living in a different era now. So how do we explain to them why these roots are still important for making sense of Quakerism and its place in a long-established prophetic tradition? And, just as importantly, how do we convey to others the possibility that our Quaker experience may have a wider relevance to the evolution of Christianity in the decades to come, as more and more people reject a doctrinal basis to religious faith?

As part of the commitment to honesty and plain speaking, Friends are usually very careful about how things are described. I know that naming our central practice meeting for *worship* now raises questions for some Friends. They ask whether it is still an accurate description of what people are doing when we gather in silence, if significant numbers of those present do not think in terms of a God who can be worshipped, or that what they understand by God does not require our worship. Integrity to the Quaker way requires us to express our faith in language that allows for our varied spiritual understandings. We need to be faithful to our collective aspiration; our experience of sharing something more than individual meditation or *being quiet together*. Whatever language we use, my sense of the essence of Quaker worship, and of our decision-making, is a willing surrender to something greater than and beyond our everyday selves.

I have been greatly helped to an inclusive understanding of Quaker worship by these words of Buddhist teacher Kevin Griffin: "It's not important how we understand God, but rather that we have a sense of that which is greater than us, the wonder of creation, of consciousness; the miracle of the loving heart, of the innocent child; the joy of exploring the inner life; the marvel of engaging the world."[6] As Friends we wait expectantly upon an essentially mysterious Reality, which is greater than us, trusting it will guide us – both in our personal lives and collectively as a faith community. While we allow one another considerable freedom in how we may imagine this greater power, and recognise that no words or image can ever adequately express its nature, both Quaker tradition and our personal experience testify to its

6 Kevin Griffin, *One Breath at a Time: Buddhism and the Twelve Steps* (Emmaus, PA: Rodale Press, 2004), p.68.

reality. This, in my view, is the bare minimum of our common Quaker faith; of what we share, in our diversity, within the skin of the Quaker banana, and I cannot see anything less than that as having integrity, as doing justice to both our history and our continuing evolution as a faith community. What is important is the way we draw on this sense of a greater power underlying our faith – through commitment to spiritual growth, to self-forgetting and self-transcendence expressed as witness in the world. Commitment to the Quaker way, a way rooted in Christianity and open to new light, is ultimately what defines the skin of the Quaker banana, what marks us out as the Religious Society of Friends.

Further reading

Quaker Faith & Practice: The book of Christian discipline of the Yearly Meeting of the Religious Society of Friends (Quakers) in Britain (London: Britain Yearly Meeting, 4th edition, 2009) provides helpful background reading about Quakerism, both historical and contemporary. *Advices & Queries*, while also published separately, is the first section. Pink Dandelion, *The Quakers: A very short introduction* (Oxford: Oxford University Press, 2008) gives a sense of the diversity of Friends worldwide and includes recommendations for further reading, particularly on Quaker history. *Listening Spirituality* by Patricia Loring; Vol. 1, *Personal Spiritual Practices Among Friends* and Vol. 2, *Corporate Spiritual Practice Among Friends* (Washington Grove, MD: Openings Press, 1997 and 1999) both draw widely from Christian and other faith traditions with suggestions for further reading and resources. *Living the Way: Quaker spirituality and community* (2nd ed., London: Quaker Books, 2003) by Ursula Jane O'Shea is a valuable short text that gives an overview of the Quaker spiritual heritage and key issues that Friends face today.

Timothy Ashworth

For those interested in the experience of meditation in the Christian tradition I describe, among other books recommended by Patricia Loring are *The Art of Prayer: An Orthodox anthology* (London: Faber, 1997) and Abhishiktananda, *Prayer* (Norwich: Canterbury Press, 2006).

Information about Andrew Cohen and the magazine that he founded can be found at: www.enlightennext.org

For a rich presentation of the prophetic nature of early Quaker experience, Douglas Gwyn's *Apocalypse of the Word: The life and message of George Fox* (Richmond, IN: Friends United Press, 1986) remains the book to turn to.

Michael Sheeran's *Beyond Majority Rule: Voteless decisions in the Religious Society of Friends* (Philadelphia: Philadelphia Yearly

Meeting, 1983) gives what is still an illuminating view of Quaker discernment processes seen by a sympathetic outsider. Both are usually obtainable from the Quaker Bookshop at Friends House, London. *Quaker Faith & Practice* contains much material on both the meaning and exercise of Quaker discernment.

The New Revised Standard Version of the Bible uses inclusive language but is also in a line of translations going back to the Authorised Version. It includes the "faith of" translation of Paul in a footnote each time it occurs. This interpretation of Paul is particularly associated with the scholar Richard B. Hays (*The Faith of Jesus* [SBLDS, 56]; Chico, CA: Scholars Press, 1983), but a more accessible work that uses it is Luke Timothy Johnson, *The Writings of the New Testament* (3rd ed., London: SPCK, 2010). This is a major resource not least because each chapter ends with a substantial bibliographical note. Two scholars from different approaches to Jesus, Marcus J. Borg and N.T. Wright, engage respectfully together in *The Meaning of Jesus* (London: SPCK, 1999). For that reason it is a helpful way of getting a sense of the variety of scholarship on Jesus and how different approaches affect the conclusions scholars come to. Those wanting to explore my presentation of Paul are directed to Timothy Ashworth, *Paul's Necessary Sin: The experience of liberation* (Aldershot: Ashgate, 2006).

Alex Wildwood

The best source on the shift from religion to spirituality is David Tacey, *The Spirituality Revolution: The emergence of contemporary spirituality* (Hove: Brunner-Routledge, 2004); but see also John Drane, *Do Christians Know How to be Spiritual? The rise of new spirituality and the mission of the Church* (London: Darton, Longman & Todd, 2005), particularly Chapter 1, and Harvey Gillman's *Consider the Blackbird: Reflections on spirituality and language* (London: Quaker Books, 2007). Of the huge number of titles published on the subject of spirituality, I recommend Ursula King's *The Search for Spirituality: Our global quest for meaning and fulfillment* (Norwich: Canterbury Press, 2009), Wayne Teasdale's *The Mystic Heart: Discovering a universal spirituality in the world's religions* (Novato, CA: New World Library, 2001) and Roger Walsh, *Essential Spirituality: The 7 central practices to awaken heart and mind* (New York: Wiley, 1999).

For those approaching Christianity again for the first time (or coming to it anew) I suggest Christian mystic Jim Marion's *The Death of the Mythic God: The rise of evolutionary spirituality* (Charlottesville, VA: Hampton Roads Publishing, 2004) and John Selby's *Jesus for the Rest of Us* (Hampton Roads, 2006). In moving from "faith in" to "faith of", I have found Buddhist Sharon Salzberg's *Faith: Trusting your own deepest experience* (London: Element/HarperCollins, 2002) invaluable, while Tom Stella's informative guide to the spiritual life, *The God Instinct: Heeding your heart's unrest* (Notre Dame, IN: Sorin Books, 2001) is full of warmth, lived experience and practical wisdom.

Of the large number of books on addiction/recovery, I particularly recommend Gerald G. May, *Addiction & Grace: Love and spirituality in the healing of addictions* (New York: HarperCollins, 1991) a comprehensive and insightful account of addiction, compulsions and attachments in general; also Kevin Griffin, *One Breath at a Time: Buddhism and the Twelve Steps* (Emmaus, PA: Rodale Press, 2004). Griffin is a Buddhist teacher and recovering alcoholic who writes with great honesty and compassion about spiritual sickness and the journey back to wholeness. To read more about how my own diverse spiritual experiences link with being a Friend, see Alex Wildwood, *A Faith to Call Our Own: Quaker tradition in the light of contemporary movements of the Spirit* (London: Quaker Home Service, 1999).

Further resources

Resources and material to support groups and individuals working with this book will be found at:

www.woodbrooke.org.uk/spiritualdiversity

For information on other courses and resources, contact:

Woodbrooke Quaker Study Centre
1046 Bristol Road, Birmingham B29 6LJ
Tel: 0121 472 5171
Email: enquiries@woodbrooke.org.uk
Website: www.woodbrooke.org.uk

Other works mentioned in this book

Rex Ambler, *Truth of the Heart* (London: Quaker Books, 2001).
William Bloom, *Soulution: The holistic manifesto* (Carlsbad, CA, and London: Hay House Inc., 2004)

David Boulton, ed., *Godless for God's Sake* (Dent: Dales Historical Monographs, 2006).

Callum Brown, *The Death of Christian Britain: Understanding secularisation 1800–2000* (London: Routledge, 2001).

Jeremy Carrette & Richard King, *Selling Spirituality: The silent takeover of religion* (London: Routledge, 2005).

Charles Carter, *On Having a Sense of All Conditions* (London: Friends Home Service Committee, 1971).

Deepak Chopra, *The Third Jesus: How to find truth and love in today's world* (London: Rider, 2008) Jasmin Lee Cori, *The Tao of Contemplation: Re-sourcing the inner life* (York Beach, ME: Samuel Weiser, 2000).

Don Cupitt et al., *Time & Tide: Sea of Faith beyond the millennium* (Winchester: O Books, 2001).

Edgar G. Dunstan, *Quakers and the Religious Quest* (London: George Allen & Unwin, 1956).

Jeni Edwards, *The New Age and the Church* (Youlgrave, Derbyshire: Bumblebee Booklets, 1992).

David Elkins, *Beyond Religion: 8 alternative paths to the sacred* (Wheaton, IL: Quest Books, 1998).

Robert Forman, *Grassroots Spirituality: What it is, why it's here, where it's going* (Exeter: Imprint Academic, 2004)

George Fox, *Journal*, ed. John Nickalls (Cambridge: Cambridge University Press, 1952).

Dag Hammarskjöld, *Markings* (London: Faber & Faber, 1966).

Alistair Heron, Ralph Hetherington and Joseph Pickvance, *The State of the Yearly Meeting: Where do we seem to be,* (London: Quaker Home Service and Woodbrooke, 1994)

Francis Howgill, *Francis Howgill's Testimony concerning Edward Burrough*, in Edward Burrough, *The Memorable Works of a Son of Thunder and Consolation*, 1672.

John Lampen *Finding the Words: Quaker experience and language* (the author, 21 Heathfield Gardens, Stourbridge DY8 3YD).

Jim Marion, *The Death of the Mythic God: The rise of evolutionary spirituality* (Charlottesville, VA: Hampton Roads, 2004).

Bel Mooney, *Devout Sceptics: Conversations about faith and doubt* (London: Hodder & Stoughton, 2003).

David Robert Ord, *Your Forgotten Self Mirrored in Jesus the Christ* (Vancouver: Namaste Publishing, 2007).

Further reading

William Penn, *The Peace of Europe, the Fruits of Solitude, and other Writings*, ed. Edwin B. Bronner, (London: Everyman, 1993).

John Selby, *Jesus for the Rest of Us* (Charlottesville, VA: Hampton Roads, 2006)

Philip Sheldrake, *A Brief History of Spirituality* (Oxford: Blackwell, 2007)

Adrian B. Smith, *God, Energy & the Field* (Winchester: O Books, 2008).

John Shelby Spong, *Jesus for the Non-Religious* (New York: Harper, 2007).

Douglas V. Steere, *Mutual Irradiation: A Quaker view of ecumenism* (Wallingford, PA: Pendle Hill Publications, 1971).

Who We Are: Questions of Quaker identity, Booklet A: Our Tradition and Today (London: Quaker Home Service and Woodbrooke, 1995)

Alex Wildwood, "Tradition & Transition: Opening to the sacred yesterday and today", *Woodbrooke Journal*, Winter 2001, No 9.

N. T. Wright, *The Resurrection of the Son of God* (London: SPCK, 2003).